Praise for *In Honor of the Feminine: Jungian Analysts and the Complexities of Love*

I love the book—badly needed in these days of patriarchal chaos. Analysts tell better stories, and these Jungian analysts share remarkable personal stories of love and Eros. These dig deep into the mythic heritage of the feminine; one open to men as well as women if they have the wisdom to read with the soul. In this book find troubled Psyche, Persephone in the underworld, mermaids, sea goddesses, tortured Medusa, and more, in dialogue with animus figures who may be stunted by, or liberated from, patriarchy. Here the personal is political, archetypal, potent. It provides rich fertile ground for anyone who seeks the feminine or any of Her gifts, divine relationships, or relationship with the divine. Read this book and you are helping Her return to the world that cannot live without Her.

– Susan Rowland, author of the Mary Wandwalker mysteries and *Jung: A Feminist Revision*

This book is a true gift, a gift that must not be read with one's eyes but, as Cyrano de Bergerac would do, with one's lips, with one's heart.

Through these profound, moving, brave, beautiful auto-biographical stories, the authors—eight women, eight analysts—have once again reminded me that knowledge and meaning are not just forms of understanding and explaining. In fact, a true meaning must always entail a redemption from the difficulties, the setbacks, even the dismays of our lives and, above all, from the dark allures of nihilism. The redemption that this kind of meaning makes possible, and that so beautifully moves this book deep from within, is the transformation of the tragic nature of life into beauty and freedom through compassion and love. These eight stories in *honor of feminine lives* are testaments of this.

Some books are good books, some may be very good, but it is a very rare occasion to read a book and to feel overwhelmed with *gratitude*. I do feel moved and grateful for the depth, honesty, wisdom, and, above everything else, for the redeeming, transformative love of these testimonies, these eight wonderful stories. Their literary fabric—which sometimes reminded me of my beloved Alice Munro or Kent Haruf—is made of the shining emotional substance through which every analyst and patient weave together the threads of their stories through memory, to redeem the tragedy of life into beauty.

The memories, feelings, and reflections that the authors share so intimately with us transcend the love of which they are made into a spiritual testament and make of this book a must that any analyst—anyone— should read.

– Stefano Carta, professor of Dynamic Psychology and Ethnopsychology at the University of Cagliari, Italy; past president of the *Italian Association of Analytical Psychology* and past co-editor for Europe of the *Journal of Analytical Psychology*, author of *The Infinite Ladder,* Routledge

These are the voices we have been waiting for. We feel we know these women and, though each story is profoundly unique, they are also us. We can relate!

Life changes sometimes in a flash, an event, or a startling awareness. And sometimes it changes at a slow roll until clarity reveals itself, the path opens, and we seize the opportunity offered to us for a new view and a more meaningful life.

These women, Jungian analysts, generously share deeply and personally from their own depths; stories of feeling lost, unmoored, betrayed, "messed up," vulnerable and brokenhearted. Jung reminds us that early on we find we get "caught and entangled in aimless experiences, and the judging intellect with its categories proves itself powerless." (CW 9i, par. 66) .... So then what? The authors share a way through dreams, unexpected encounters, myths, and artistic expression that, if we can allow the brokenness and accept the descent, an inner life, the presence of Psyche will guide us.

This is a tribute to all who find love in the wounded places. We hear in these stories of love which survives, with open eyes, the grief and crushing pain of the human condition. Of love which rises, reconstructed from the ashes of defeat and betrayals. We hear of love that burns on in the rubble of the broken heart. We are assured of a love that nourishes in the center of the greatest vulnerability. And it is our love too, within each of us; it belongs to us, and we will honor the feminine who will accompany and guide us along the serpentine path of self-discovery. It is the sacred feminine who will hold the space for us to live again, to continue on, to surprise us, and ultimately, to "Love."

This is a book for men who, through the lens of the feminine, see all that they can be, and of course for women who honor the ever-evolving mystery of the feminine and the sisterhood of those who are brave enough to share their stories.

– Anne Pickup, LCMFT, Jungian analyst, Washington D.C.

This book is a profound, courageous, and compelling exploration of the archetypal feminine and its transformative power through the lens of the lives of Jungian analysts. Through deeply personal narratives, these women share their struggles, revelations, and the healing that comes from engaging deeply with the unconscious and the shadow. Themes of societal and patriarchal constraint, love, sexuality, spirituality, and individuation weave through these stories, offering readers a rich tapestry of insight into the divine feminine and how it is experienced in the lives of modern women.

– Christina Becker, Jungian analyst, author of *Soul-Making, A Journey of Resilience and Spiritual Rediscovery* and *The Heart of the Matter: Individuation as an Ethical Process*

This book is a rare treasure. The reader is invited to glimpse inside the lives of eight Jungian analysts—all of them women—as they share transformational stories of meetings with the archetypal feminine. This text offers a chance to learn from professionals who are highly experienced in guiding others through the realms of the psyche—only this time they are describing their own life experiences of meeting love, vulnerability, awe, and mystery, as well as confronting the shadow. I highly recommend this book to anyone wishing to deepen their relationships with self and other.

– Mary-Jayne Rust, Jungian Psychoanalyst, author of *Towards an Ecopsychotherapy*, Confer Books and co-editor of *Vital Signs: Psychological Responses to Ecological Crisis, Karnac Books*

These stories from women trained in listening to self-experience through a Jungian lens give the reader the primary experiential material out of which a feminine self is constructed. It is liberating to have this account of a key part of psyche they have come to know and honor. Theirs is a text that all of us can learn from.

– John Beebe, author of *Integrity in Depth*

These individuation stories of relatedness and love are told by eight women—all Jungian analysts—who name and honor the manifestations of the divine feminine in the unfolding of their lives. Edited by Jungian Analyst Marilyn Marshall, these deeply moving stories embody a variety of experiences of psyche's journey that call us all to recognize and embrace the re-valuation of the archetypal feminine against the tide of cultural constriction.

I identified with many of these stories. I think this book should be read by candidates in our training programs so that they may see what individuation looks like.

– Mary Dougherty, MFA, ATRBC, Jungian Psychoanalyst, Member of the Chicago Society of Jungian Analysts

In this wonderful collection, eight women who are Jungian analysts courageously, honestly, and openly reflect deeply on the many ways love has shaped their lives. The book lifts the veil behind which lie the mysteries of the feminine soul on its journey to find itself. It incorporates the erotic as part of the expression of love but it penetrates beyond to offer an expansive view of how Eros guides the female soul to maturity and to the freedom that comes from living more truthfully and fully in the world. Further, this is a book not just for women but also for men who wish to further their understanding of the women in their lives, and of how Eros lives within themselves.

– Steve Eliezer Zemmelman, M.S.W., Ph.D., Jungian Adult and Child Psychoanalyst, Associate Clinical Professor of Psychiatry at University of California San Francisco, adjunct professor at Pacifica Graduate Institute, member of the C. G. Jung Institute of San Francisco and the Inter-Regional Society for Jungian Analysts

How rare to be given the opportunity to accompany eight Jungian analysts—all women—on their paths to dig deep in the Psyche and find their authentic feminine roots. Each woman shares her journey through wounding, hurting, and healing to transformation and discovers her unique voice—a voice which is personal and which also reaches into the depths of the archetypal feminine energy. By telling their stories, which include the struggle with the dominant patriarchal power and facing the shadows of anger, resentment, and fear, these women show that courage, faith, and hope and a way of renewal is possible for both women and men. Read the book and come along on the adventure of Love.

– Linda Schierse Leonard, Ph.D., Jungian Analyst, author of *The Wounded Woman: Healing the Father-Daughter Relationship* (and six other books)

Among its many treasures this book is a great gift to men as a window into the hearts and psyches of women and the living reality of the feminine, both of which will undoubtedly and hopefully remain something of a mystery to us men forever.

– Thomas Singer, MD, author of *A Field Guide to American Cultural Complexes: The Battleground of the Splintered American Psyche*

In Honor of the Feminine

Jungian Analysts and the Complexities of Love

In Honor of the Feminine

Jungian Analysts and the Complexities of Love

Marilyn Marshall, Editor

CHIRON PUBLICATIONS • ASHEVILLE, NORTH CAROLINA

www.ChironPublications.com

Interior and cover design by Danijela Mijailovic
Printed primarily in the United States of America.
The cover image for this publication was created using artificial intelligence (AI) technology based on a dream of Marilyn Marshall's, the series editor. The final cover design was selected, edited, and approved by the series editor and the publisher.

ISBN 978-1-68503-645-4 paperback
ISBN 978-1-68503-646-1 hardcover
ISBN 978-1-68503-647-8 electronic
ISBN 978-1-68503-648-5 limited edition paperback
ISBN 978-1-68503-649-2 limited edition hardcover

Library of Congress Cataloging-in-Publication Data Pending

Dedication

To women and those who love them

Acknowledgments

Carl Jung's integrity and courage, his tireless depth of work and sacrifice along his individual and very human path towards wholeness—his confrontation with the unconscious, relatedness to the complex inner world of the archetypes and his love for the soul—has left a rich and fertile legacy from which I have greatly benefited and for which I'm deeply grateful.

My heartfelt appreciation for Constance, Carolyn, Nancy, Susan, Janice, Barbara, and Jacqueline, who have shared these pivotal stories in their journeys of individuation. They generously reveal their vulnerabilities, psychic landscapes, and the tensions of life rife with "madness," creativity, and meaning. Each of these women has graciously responded with openness, collaboration, and wisdom when I've relied on her perspective. It has been a privilege.

I am also especially thankful for Karen Farley, who has provided a meticulous focus of technical skill in the copy editing, proofing, and formatting of the manuscript and images for this book, as well as offering her perceptive feedback for clarification in the stories. She has been a welcome, steadfast voice of resources, knowledge, and support, and I feel fortunate to have received her patience and invaluable help during this creative process.

Many thanks to Leonard Cruz and Steve Buser, chief editors of Chiron Publications, who believed the book deserved publication, and to Chiron's Jennifer Fitzgerald, who proficiently managed the production of the book (and my many questions and emails). Additionally, I am sincerely appreciative of the women and men we asked to read the book and to consider writing an endorsement; their remarks have been included.

And finally, to the beloved family and friends who have challenged and confronted, encouraged and supported me—I am so grateful for the complexities of our love.

CONTENTS

List of Illustrations

Introduction

Marilyn Marshall

> *This play that I witnessed is my play, not your play. It is my secret, not yours. You cannot imitate me ... and my mysteries are inviolable, they belong to me and cannot belong to you. You have your own.*
> *He who enters into his own must grope through what lies at hand.... He must embrace the worthless and the worthy with the same love. (Jung, 2009, p. 246)*

In April, 2024, I shared the idea for this book with colleagues, martinis in hand as evening fell at the Inter-Regional Society of Jungian Analysts conference hotel bar in Santa Fe. The energy of the book's theme—female analysts' stories of pivotal experiences in life—guided us down into an intimate space of vulnerability, openness, and trust. We shared the struggles that awakened us to inner others that invited or demanded acknowledgment and conscious relationship. These stories circled around the topics of Eros, love, and relatedness to ourselves and others. I had been having dreams about the possibility of the book during the two previous years of pondering its value and purpose—one dream in particular right before the conference, which precipitated my bringing it up with these friends. We left that conversation touched and enriched by one another's stories.

Six weeks later, during the annual June retreat for the New Orleans Jungian Seminar, the analysts and participants had a memorial service for Del McNeely, beloved colleague and faculty member. I shared with the group a paragraph from the Prologue of her memoir, *A Russian Lullaby*, which captured Del's warmth, her "lullaby's" purpose, her open arms to life, and her Baba-Yaga-like wisdom: She briefly stated her story's purpose as "to contribute something, however small, to the understanding of a woman's feelings and thoughts about pregnancy, and to contribute something, however small, to the understanding of Russia's journey" (McNeely, 2012, p. 5). The memorial for Del following the conference discussion of pivotal experiences felt like a synchronistic encouragement for offering to the Jungian community and those interested in Jung's analytical psychology such a book as this one. So, I contacted colleagues and requested a personal story of relatedness, Eros—of the significance of love.

In Honor of the Feminine: Jungian Analysts and the Complexities of Love is the compilation of the stories of eight female analysts that have deeply affected our feminine identities and our paths of individuation. These individual experiences, as Jung comments regarding his own, are each analyst's inviolate mysteries and their revelations of love. When we gathered on Zoom to discuss writing our contributions for this book, we found ourselves in the realm of the archetypal feminine—sharing memories of *her* emergence and demands in our lives. Not only did we want to give voice to her call and authority, we wanted to lay shameless claim to the repressed and rejected aspects of her character.

Our stories honor meaningful encounters and vital dreams that span the heartbeats of childhood, adolescence, midlife, and older age. They reveal the complexities in claiming one's feminine nature through responding to the inner and outer realities of life. Collective ideals, religious beliefs, and parental expectations impact each of us. Lovers' explorations, marriage vows, family obligations, and professional detours make their marks. Sexuality, spirituality, emotional tensions, and laborious decisions have challenged us, and we have suffered through the transformational processes of becoming conscious of ourselves.

Necessity dictates the recognition of a rigidly formulated, devalued feminine legacy and its imprint on our personal mothers' attitudes and values. Although fortunately smudged over the last century by women incensed by patriarchy's proscriptions, such imprints are emblematic of an obstructed, tenuous, or neglected relationship to a divine, archetypal feminine principle. With such qualities relegated to the unconscious, the wholeness of a woman's conscious feminine identity and the processes of transformation such qualities initiate remain in the shadows. The ongoing suspicion and devaluation of the feminine has not only affected women's sense of self but, naturally, a man's capacity for relatedness to women and to his inner feminine, his anima.

Necessity also requires our confrontation with the archetypal masculine in its provocatively negative and positive attributes and effects. Unsurprisingly, our personal experiences of these archetypal qualities, evident throughout these stories, are engendered by collective patriarchal structures and attitudes and portrayed and illuminated by fathers, brothers, and male figures of familial and communal life who are living their own tensions of masculine and feminine mysteries. Both this archetype's destructive characteristics and constructive qualities reside with the inner masculine of a woman, the animus, that we avoid at our peril and face to promote our development.

Individually, we grapple with loving the worthy *and* the worthless, the unlived aspects of the personality that offer more of ourselves to us—not an easy task. Jung's statement quoted above was his reflective response following the horror of realizing he had to learn to love the bloodthirsty, blind Salome, who had professed her love for him. For Jung, she was an unwelcome and abhorrent experience of what he would come to recognize as the archetype of the anima and an emblem of his undeveloped feeling, his Eros and relatedness to the feminine. While it is true that Jung's mysteries are his and we each have our own, the Spirit of the Depths remarked to Jung that his fear of this murderous image of the feminine was his recognition of her "divine power" (Jung, 2009, p. 246).

We invite the reader to journey with us through these pivotal stories of our individual experiences with the mysteries of the psyche, the manifestation of the divine archetypal feminine, and our relationships to archetypal masculine realities. Writing was a vulnerable task of disclosure that required a solitary dedication from each of us, and we believe the value of this work will contribute to an understanding of the individuation process for women and a compassion for the complexities of love.

New Orleans, Louisiana
May, 2025

Candles in the Sea

Constance Romero

My twelfth year was ... a fateful one for me.... I was taking the long road to school ... when suddenly ... I had the overwhelming impression of having just emerged from a dense cloud. I knew all at once: now I am myself!... I came upon myself. Previously I had existed, too, but everything had merely happened to me. Now I happened to myself. (Jung, 1961/1989, p. 30; pp. 32-33)

I am an orphan, alone; nevertheless I am found everywhere.... I am youth and old [woman] at one and the same time.... I have had to be fetched out of the deep like a fish.... (Jung, 1961/1989, p. 227)

Whenever I hear the sound of thunder, I think of my Father's voice. A baritone opera singer, he could rend the air around us with explosive blasts or rumble ominously in the distance. The black lightning he carried inside occasionally broke through his cultured persona, etching our nervous systems with his indelible sonic tattoo. The truth is, none of us would know the secret that haunted him—and finally hunted him down—until the last years of his life.

But in this story, I am twelve years old and not thinking about Father and his storms. It's Christmas, 1966, in a small town on the Gulf Coast of Florida, and Big Sister has come home from college. Petite and curvy with long, blonde hair, she rolls in like high tide, and, wherever she goes, she leaves this shimmer in her wake. I, on the other hand, am tall, wear glasses, eat like a stevedore, and have a mass of dark hair that frizzes out in all directions.

This Christmas, the family is making a pilgrimage to the Florida Keys. Little Brother and I ride with Big Sister in her VW Beetle, separated, at last, from parents. Exhilarated, we are the minions of Venus as she commandeers her chariot down sleepy two-lane blacktops. Little Brother and I open the sunroof and hang our heads out like friendly dogs. The wind rushes over our faces, blowing troubles into the rearview; this is my first taste of a new kind of freedom, scary and delicious, because I have been aching for so long to inhabit some new skin that has always been just out of reach.

Down highways and byways, we head south through sleepy St. Petersburg, Bradenton, and Sarasota with their little cinderblock hotels painted electric blue or flamingo pink. We pass shell shops, bait shops, and wild stands of jacaranda, alamander, and hibiscus. Further south, there are banana trees growing alongside those sentinels of the tropics, the palms. Date palms, royal palms, scrub and saw palmetto, the Tamiami Trail winds on and on.

Late in the day, the Seven Mile Bridge to the Keys rises to greet us, and as we pass each island in the chain, we call out their names: Marathon! Matecumbe! Key Largo! until we finally reach Islamorada and our hotel—The Key Lantern Inn, an old Florida relic with a plaster lighthouse out front. The plan is for the family to converge and go feast on oysters at a local restaurant that snags your senses in the way old seafood joints can. You know the place: A large, rusted anchor and chain stand at the entrance, and inside, fishermen's nets hang from the ceiling, cradling a harvest of dried sponges and plastic tropical fish. There is a huge, glassy-eyed swordfish mounted on an old cypress wall, flanked by autographed 8 × 10s of local celebrities and Hollywood stars. Each table features paper placemats with a map of Florida tourist attractions: Silver Springs, Cypress Gardens, Weeki Wachee, and our personal favorite, the Miami Serpentarium, run by a man bitten so many times while milking rattlers that he looks as brittle and translucent as old snakeskin.

The ruler of this eclectic domain is, however, a larger-than-life mermaid lovingly rendered on the wall of the main dining room. Voluptuous and regal, she floats, trident in one hand and a glowing candle in the other. Her red mane swirls around her body, and her silver tail, wreathed with shells, seahorses, and starfish, shimmers in the light. However, feasting with her must wait, because the parents have not yet arrived, and so we set out for some short-term refreshment.

Big Sister pulls into a ramshackle Quick Stop, though once inside, we realize things are not as they seem. The floor is a worn, cracked red cement, and there is no Icee machine, no glass cooler with cartons of milk, no wire stands filled with candy or chips. Rather, I get my first whiff of cigarettes and stale beer and, as my eyes adjust in the dim light, I see a pool table, a juke box, and an ornate wooden altar that I suddenly realize is a bar. It sits beneath a long mirror with twinkling lights and tiered rows of glass bottles. Tucked beneath its generous shelf are high stools lined up for souls seeking communion or oblivion.

After a minute, I realize with a jolt that Big Sister and I are the only females in the place as five or six young men materialize from corners and back rooms. They look us up and down and circle up. Shirts hanging open, they emit a feral mix of suntan oil and gasoline. All skinny torsos and tattoos, they are terrifying, tantalizing—*Other*. My ears ring as Mick Jagger belts from the juke, "Hey…you…get offa my cloud!" I shoot a panicked look at Big Sister but stand transfixed as she sizes them up and puffs out her fur. Seconds pass, no one speaks, and then all the light in that dingy place wends its way into the center of her and, as her shimmer passes through our retinas, the alchemy of her scent and poise washes away the predatory leanings in the room. I am limp with relief as we are suddenly met with a kind of sheepish, sad, gentle sweetness: "Miss, would you like a Co-Cola? Some peanuts? Y'all wanna play pool?" One asks my name, and I can't believe anyone has noticed me in the wake of Big Sister. When we eventually make it back to the hotel and get to dinner, it is under the munificent gaze of the mermaid that I feel a quickening in my sense of myself. I shiver as it rises inside.

Next morning we wake to find the air lies gentle on our skin, and the December sun emanates a cool white glare that washes everything but the water to the color of scoured bones. As we head toward Key West, it is all turquoise on white, turquoise on white, as we slide into another reality that is Seminole, Miccosukee, and Calusa, who know the sky and sea are shimmering cosmic mirrors of each other.

Fatefully, at a stop in Bahia Honda mid-morning, Little Brother and I get hungry, and against earlier parental admonitions, we head for a lean-to hamburger stand on the beach. Joining a line of kids our age seems as natural as the smell of the chopped onions, ketchup, and French fries that comprise the ultimate siren call to the adolescent glandular system. However, unbeknownst to us, Father has finished his exploration of the local flora and fauna and decides to pull up stakes for Key West sooner than expected. He hunts down Mother and Big Sister, asking our whereabouts. Sensing his earlier foul mood building like a thunderhead, they skitter off like two birds and hide behind a dune.

"Do you hear thunder?" I ask Little Brother. "Naw," he says. "I'm starving." But there is a subtle shift in the air, and we sense him before we see him coming. Then, like a nightmare, he is there yelling at full volume, his mouth working like the whirling blades of a giant fan. My nervous system goes into shock, moving in the slowed-down time frame that is trauma, made all the worse because of the other kids staring in horror. He grabs us by our shirts, jerks us out of line, and thunders for us to get to the car. Mother and Big Sister are waiting for us, survivor guilt written all over their faces.

As with many families, the standard protocol is to wait until the storm passes—which it will—hate him for a few hours, and then forget. And mostly we do. Key West in those days is vibrant and rough around the edges. Going into Hemingway's storied house and favorite bar with Big Sister is as novel as the Key Lime pie. Manx cats roam the streets, dodging the legs of drunken Navy sailors, and the old salts by the docks, their grimy Captain's hats askew, bark promises of a big catch. Couples openly kiss and fondle one another, oblivious to beleaguered parents trying to corral their children, high on cotton candy, madly dashing about in shorts and sunscreen. I, too, feel intoxicated; life teems and sways, in your face one minute—and just beneath the surface the question plays on repeat: "Who are *you*? What *moves* you in this raucous, unboundaried mix?" Amongst the sprawl of beauty and decay that is Key West, I am clear that I don't want to be a permanently unmoored soul taken down by forces as old as time. But, oh, I want adventure! I want a story worth telling and need to hear the stories of those who, lost and broken, find their way to safe harbor.

As the day winds down, we spy a small shop with rows of bleached sand dollars in the window. A sign proclaims they are "Nature's proof of the presence of Jesus" as each contains a small bone at its center in the shape of the Dove of Peace. Hmmm.... The sand dollars look desiccated and smell fusty too, unlike the large conch shells, whose wide, pink lips still offer the smell of the sea and the sound of waves if you press them up close. There are also postcards with photographs of women pressed into mermaid suits. They smile at the camera, exhaling bubbles in underwater grottos. Other cards tell nautical tales in vivid images, and one is of La Sirène, the Goddess of the Sea, who lights the way home for all who have drowned as well as those kidnapped from their homelands and enslaved. There are also drawings of other kinds of mermaids, some seductively luring men to death with ethereal songs, while others feature people in white flowing robes and turbans, offering flowers to the Mermaid Goddess by the shore.

I buy every postcard. This Goddess of the Sea may not be all peace and love, but she feels real, sensuous, and definitely more alive than Jesus, whose worship, for me at this point, requires church-going, guilt, and mind-numbing boredom. The crucifix I was gifted as a little girl, with its placid, well-groomed, blue-eyed Jesus (whom I fervently kissed and longed to marry) has lost its allure. By age twelve, Jesus's loving kindness had yet to make a dent in my father's rage, my mother's passivity, or my bewilderment at the lives of adults. I reveled in the capacity of the Goddess to vanquish an intrusive interloper, to save a lost soul, to free the enslaved. La Sirène, in my imagination, became the secret promise of another life, always flowing alongside this one, *unbound and unbinding*.

On the drive back to the hotel, I remain angry at my father. He crossed a line this time and has come up against that quickening inside me. I will not look at him, and by the evening I remain, to my mother's growing consternation, unforgiving. The next day he tries halfheartedly to make contact, but I can tell he wants the old terms—no acknowledgement on his part that his rage was out of line, that he could have just asked us to come back to the car. Rather, he wants to get things back the way they were and get my mother off his back. She comes and pleads, "He's really hurting … he feels bad … he knows it was wrong." But I am confused because, as usual, I cannot *see* or *feel* any of these emotions coming from him.

None of us will know, until the last years of his life, that my father's heritage is a closely guarded secret. Enfolded in a safe Episcopal facade, the incongruities of our life abound: We never eat pork, we puzzle over his antisemitic comments, and we are told that, aside from his parents, he has no living relatives. We have no idea of the fear, anguish, and pride buried in the mountain of his being, because he was, in fact, Jewish. Raised in the deep south, he was instructed by his immigrant forebears to deny the family history at all costs. When, at forty, I find out in a phone call (from a cousin I did not know existed) that we are Jewish, he tells me that, despite numerous attempts to assimilate, to be Christian, he is haunted by his childhood classmates' chant about his grandmother: "*Rebecca Cohen is a Jew, and every word you know is true*." And so, my father killed off that part of himself, struck it from the record, and brought down the wrath of a God denied upon himself and his children.

But back in 1966, I know none of this, and go to bed that night deciding that I will speak to him, but it will be to make a new arrangement between us. I don't *think* about this—it is simply knowing instinctively that I am not a child anymore and, because of this, he cannot degrade me in the old way. I can feel he knows this, too.

I fall into a restless sleep and wake at midnight. Hankering to see the water, I steal past Big Sister and head across the hotel courtyard, where a small dock beckons. I sit in a rusty pink metal chair whose springs creak as I rock back and forth, back and forth. The Gulf laps at the pilings, insects hum in the electric light slung over the pier, and the night wind rustles the palms. In the distance, fish jump and slap. I get up and go to the edge of the dock, wishing I could swim away from this painful life. Here the water is all rippling obsidian except for patches of phosphorescence that glimmer in the dark. If I dove down and down and down, maybe I would find another country, one far away that feels welcoming to someone like me. Would La Sirène guide me there? And then suddenly, barely breaking the surface tension of the water, a large fish begins to rise: So close, I see her unblinking eye as she bears up in the quiet, displaying herself slowly, gracefully, so that each section of her silver body streams in profile until the fanned tail descends. Wild with excitement at seeing a creature so big, so close, I want to shout, "See!... Look!... Did you see that?" But there is no one around, and it is I who need to *see*—that there are forces in this world, in Nature, whose beauty, sentience, and generous presence outstrips the tragedy of a Father severed from his roots.

It will take years, countless losses and boons, before this story feels ripe for the telling, before I can say to you that it was La Sirène calling me from my bed, her candles burning in the sea. *Her* way reminds my body of its ability to re-member, over and over, the gift of being heard, the miracle of being found. And that *this* is the work, our individual, ongoing struggle to keep psyche's sacred call and response alive in each of us. Old sailors know if you get too close, La Sirène can pull you in, but if you leave her gifts where the sand and the sea rise to greet each other, she may bless you, keep you, and make her face to shine upon you, even when the sound of thunder blows much of what you love to pieces. I like to dream that she lit a candle in black water, and I am back on that dock, where the lights, the palms, and the sea coral bones of my body all begin to … shimmer.

Love Letters

Carolyn Bates

Dedicated to the love of family,
in all its shapes and sizes.
It can be the light one follows out of great darkness.

August 18, 1969
Dear Lyons and Jim,
You now are the two men with whom my hands and my heart have been most closely joined, and for whom my love has been deepest. It is a joy to me, and a kind of relief, to ask that you two together, in silence if need be, but in company, speak with the Lord for me. I am not reluctant on my own account to turn loose of this life; but my heart grows heavy at the thought of leaving Virginia by herself, and of leaving Carolyn before she is of a better age. The boys are grown, and Deborah at eighteen is her own person: They can support their grief. My own prayer is that I may stay long enough to send Virginia before me, and to see Carolyn grown to the composure she will reach in a few more years.

May the Lord bless you and keep you,
Neal

*****

July 24, 1970
Dear Son,
Your letter with the copies of our wills came yesterday. What I want to write here will be an expression of our wish for the action of the guardian to Carolyn, for whom, in the event of our early demise—which again we say we do not by any means anticipate—the circumstances are complicated. Her life has been of concern to your mother and me since the doctor's diagnosis of my impairment in August 1969. Carolyn has a kind of creative nature, a need for solitude and reflection, that is wholly out of place in any urban environment, and indeed fairly out of place in this modern world altogether. If we were able, we would move into the country for her sake now.
Subsequent to our visit with Harold and Camille Lockwood last fall, and again this spring, our thoughts with respect to her became clearer and firmly directed. We asked them whether, in the event your mother and I should die, they would consider letting Carolyn live with them until she was through school. You can, I think, imagine Camille's response. She was deeply moved that we should have thought of them in this way. They are more than willing to have Carolyn and said, "Starting right now!"
Yesterday evening we talked with Carolyn about this possibility. At 15, it is not easy for her to think about our death, as you may well understand; but she did so with considerable composure. After thinking silently for quite a while, she first spoke of how you and Michael and Richard might feel about this, and then

expressed her own feelings that this is what she would really love to do, to stay with Harold and Camille in the country outside of Weatherford.
It seems foolish to express appreciation. Our love is what you have in abundance.

Dad and Mother

*****

I was a fortunate child. Born to older parents who could laugh at their imperfections, together they cultivated a spiritual and intellectual quest to live meaningful lives. They loved one another and their five children with quiet, fierce certainty, with anxieties about our well-being, and with bemusement and curiosity about our minds and character. Their letters, spanning fifty years, narrate the arc of their lives and those of their children. Their letters convey a deep appreciation, wonder, and respect for the reality of their children's inner lives and outer interests: our naïve and studied passions, our own anxieties, our temperaments. I am, to this day, indebted to the early years they shepherded, grateful for their deliberate respect for my introversion. They appeared to know it was theirs to protect. My recall, and their writings, paint a picture of two people who felt no compulsion to overdirect my early life with concerns about social engagements and developmental expectations. I was free to roam, Mowgli-like, in what at the time seemed like a massive backyard. Amidst the perfume of blossoming orange and grapefruit trees, I was free to build my forts and doorways into imaginary worlds, free to bring home the handful of stray curs that roamed the dusty streets of our Laredo neighborhood, free to lose myself in unending hours of solitary play, and always, always free to engage an inner world.

*****

For most of my life I have known myself to be in the hands of the Lord, and I am certainly no less so now than in more promising days. The doctors, I think, have no hope at all for my recovery, at least they offer me none. But like Cyrano de Bergerac, I have no surrender in me, and will flail about with my puny sword, to the last awkward stroke, if it comes to that—not as fighting an enemy, but simply as not giving up a contest.

Neal Craig, 1970

*****

May 14, 1971
21 months after diagnosis, at home.
I stood clasping my father's lightly blanketed feet. Standing vigil with my brothers and sister, we watched as our mother, sitting on the edge of my father's deathbed, gently stroked his face. My father's eyes—all that he could still control of his ALS-ravaged body, slowly rounded the circle, taking in each one of us: my brother Richard, who would become our rock, at his left side, my brother Michael, beside him, my sister Debbie, close by my side, my eldest brother Gerald, his hands on my mother's shoulders, and my mother, upon whom my father's gaze came to rest. She held his gaze until the last fading spark of light and life took its leave. After some moments, Michael slowly reached forward and closed my father's eyes.

And I thought, "*Not yet. Please.*"

*****

What is the measure by which you measure yourself?
Neal Craig, February 8, 1968

*****

Perhaps it was a Hestia presence, woven by a father and mother both working from home. I don't, from those earliest years, remember a time when they were not there. I have wondered how this inchoate knowing—unspoken, unthought—that I was watched over, anchored itself in me. Certainly, there was always an open window or a screen door through which a parent or older sibling could listen or look to check on my well-being. It is only decades later, in sifting through their letters, that I have come to understand—and feel immense gratitude for—the attitudes with which they both watched over their children. I, the youngest, knew in those early years—felt in those early years—that others were there for me, responsive to my needs, rarely intruding, simply allowing me … space. Space to imagine, space to play, space to find the stories that would be ready once I mastered the alphabet.

*****

Being a Christian is a way of life. You can be a better Christian when you're in a good church. And you can be a better Christian when you're not in a bad church.
Neal Craig, April 14, 1963

*****

This is not to say that our lives were free of hardship. Financial hardship was there; religious fundamentalism, with its trans-generational undercurrents of shame and fear, abounded in the community that my parents navigated. Undercurrents of my mother's anxiety manifested at times through her worried sharpness. Wheels within cultural wheels, none of which I was aware, spun about the household at the corner of Chihuahua and Malinche. Ours was a preacher's family in a small Protestant denomination, surrounded by a sea of Catholicism. But within these small, independent churches that stretched across Texas, I would later come to understand—through the paper trail of letters that is my inheritance—how my parents became the targets of a poisonous streak of envy coursing through the letter-writing world, as a small handful of brethren found my father's open-hearted and grace-oriented sermons far too threatening, far too daring. The fact of my mother having fled an abusive marriage and divorced before meeting and eventually marrying my father could never be overlooked. They eventually left what had to be an intolerable affiliation in a church they experienced as rife with bitterness and back-biting and, with a small handful of beloved friends, strove to build a "good" church, first meeting in our small home. Land would be found, a loan guaranteed, a small building erected. A new, more open-minded church was born. We sat on the second row on the right, on dark hardwood pews my father and brothers built, and I took in my father's quiet sermons: charity, grace, patience, fellowship, and an invitation always to hold fast to love.

*****

February, 1968
18 months before the first symptoms of ALS.
We had left the Texas/Mexico border for Austin, where my father enrolled in university to study linguistics. Unaware of the financial strain my parents shouldered, I found home to be a sanctuary, each of us reading our favorite—or required—texts: for myself, Tolkien; for my sister, mysteries and microbiology. My mother drank in the

writings of C. S. Lewis, my father, Faulkner. And we talked about them all.

I was twelve when I came home from school and found my father sitting on the edge of their bed. He was pensive, and I sat next to him, cuddling my hand in his, and asked him what was wrong. He shared a dream he had had while napping:

> *We were flying, my father, mother, sister and I, through Narnia. Wearing long white robes, we could look down below us and see all the forests and the hills. We followed a river as we flew toward a bridge ahead of us that spanned the river. As we flew under the bridge, my father's robe got caught on the truss. He struggled to free himself, but couldn't, and the three of us had to fly on without him.*

The poignancy of this dream burned into my mind and memory. There's not a Jungian reading this who wouldn't think, "Ah! A dream of fear of loss and separation from those whom one loves. A dream of transition, baptism, and transformation. A dream calling one to come back to earth … and just what is a grown man thinking sharing a troubling dream with a twelve-year-old?" Only our family shared dreams—usually funny ones from our parents, which made us laugh, and scary ones from the children, which they comforted us away from. It is only in hindsight, which Jung notes is the only position from which one can suggest that a dream is prognostic, that I understand that my father's unconscious knew what his body did not. Not yet.

*****

May 19, 1971
Dearest father and mother Pearl,
It was hard leaving you looking so forlorn and desolate

as we drove away Sunday. My whole scope of living—and I know yours—looks bleak and so terribly empty. They tell me time and occupation will make the pain go away.
But I will never stop missing Neal.

Virginia

*****

June 8, 1971
Dear Floyd,
Loneliness for Neal is almost excruciating at times. I am trying to remember all the words I've spoken to others in similar circumstances and am finding to recall them doesn't much help. One such wrote advising me simply to endure—gradually one must make the struggle to reenter living. For the nonce, I feel drained of all joy. At the moment I feel not fearful of dying but fearful of living. But living does go on. Carolyn's distress comes out in asthma and nightmares. Asthma seems to be controlled at the moment, but she still has haunting dreams of her dad, and confusing (symbolic) ones like being driven or forced into a room of many doors and becoming frantic in not knowing which door will let her out....

Virginia

*****

It is sometimes aggravating, after a lifetime of having a voice that was an obedient servant in almost every respect, to have it now come out almost any old way, and then reluctantly.

Neal, December 1, 1970

*****

It is a near-lethal combination: having a good father leave too soon, having a mother bereft. It is a precipitous moment in a life not yet fully anchored in itself. The potential for composure my father saw in me began to erode in indiscernible degrees, though I held my ground for two years, sustained in large part by a caring family, devoted school teachers, and an enveloping, loving group of friends. I look back and see the care and affection of so many who held me in those last years of high school: the Latin teacher who drew me aside to assure me she was there if I needed to talk, the church youth group who circled ranks around me, the kindness of the church elders when I went to them soon after my father died, asking that they change the word "shut-ins" to describe homebound parishioners. I could not, I explained, abide thinking of my father as having been "shut-in" even as the degenerative disease of Amyotrophic Lateral Sclerosis had slowly closed the door to his mobility and his life of teaching. A soul couldn't be "shut-in," nor could a spirit. They complied in the most loving of ways and began using a different word: homebound. The power of a single word was not lost on me. Nor the power of bringing a single voice to the table. I was determined to hold onto my voice, hoping it would, when joined with other voices, carry me through.

*****

> *A great deal of living has loneliness in it, even in the middle of a crowd or in the bosom of a family, and a number of us seek out that loneliness, but this is so*

very different from feelings of desolation. Those are different things.

Neal Craig, December 26, 1969

Persephone's Descent

Those things we fear are those things we shall, in fearing them, become.

Carolyn, 1975

Sorrow

Carolyn, 1972

How does one reach escape velocity from grief? I couldn't find the formula. At eighteen, my descent began as I felt myself dragged into a depressive isolation, falling away from my sense of self, my feet no longer on solid ground. My friend, solitude, could not offer me its familiar solace, and desolation indeed took its place. As college awaited, each friend who had held me set out for conservative colleges steeped in fundamentalism. It felt like a diaspora, but I couldn't follow them. I couldn't bring myself to attend these Christian colleges, feeling a claustrophobia I couldn't understand when visiting their campuses. I felt a worry I couldn't articulate; that there would have been attempts to cull a way of thinking that had awakened in me, that my inner world would have been given no truck, no ambit, other than what fundamentalism dictated women should think, be, and feel. It was a path too narrow and too narrow-minded. But the wider path held such tremendous pitfalls, and I had no clue how to navigate them.

*****

For me—in my youth—I did not know sexual drive was what it is—only a restlessness within me that I could not understand.

Virginia, 1977
Talk given to the Ladies' Bible Class

*****

There are so many ways vulnerability manifests in youth. If only I could have let myself talk with my mother, to understand my own "restlessness within me." A father's daughter without a father, my descent tumbled me through a series of transferences onto too many of the young men whose paths I crossed. ("Are *you* my father?") Of course, each relationship failed, the unconscious ask was impossible to meet. Despite—for some—their best efforts, the safe havens I sought in these relationships eluded me. The sense of belonging I had known in my earliest years—despite my family's never budging in their love for me—began to erode. No relationship could quiet the grief, nor fill the emptiness, nor offer direction.

Did Persephone know these things? I think she must have. I think she must have known an unspeakable grief and loneliness born of separation. My worried family, from whom I was shutting myself out, supported my decision to get psychological help, and the most difficult yet life-changing transference actually arrived where one might most expect it to.

*****

Remember Hemingway: "The world breaks every one and afterward many are strong at the broken places." (Hemingway, 1929, p. 264)

Carolyn, 1975

When a good man has to leave before he can teach a daughter what a bad man is, how does she recognize the destructive masculine? At nineteen, I hadn't known to call it depression. I didn't know there was a name for the uncertainty, the anxiety, the night terrors and gripping loss that had taken possession. I have long wondered at the turn of fate at that moment in my life. For Persephone, Hades was both a place and a person. Already in the underworld of depression, I would go on to meet the abductor when—of all the therapists in the city, the psychologist whose consulting room I entered would prove to have an ongoing pattern of sexually exploiting his patients.

Unworldly, naïve, unable to even imagine that a person who deemed to care for me would not have my best interest at heart, I was one of many women who fell prey to his sexual grooming and exploitation. It was the most shadowed and conflicted time of my life. My complicity was born of a wish to please, a longing to be known once again by a father, an unwillingness to challenge his assertion that this would, he assured, help me break free of my depression and shed feelings of guilt for having sexual wants. This would help me release my shame for defying the repressive edicts of Christian conservatism. (I'd never heard this choice—that one was either chaste or one was Jezebel—discussed in my father's sermons or in family conversation, but it was present in the very milieu of the church.) The irony of this relationship was the loss of another father, albeit a perverse one. And yet, the presence of a perverted father figure—by such stark contrast to the many loving men I had known in my life—helped me to wake up to the self-harm of collusion; helped me take my first steps to be a good father to myself. I began to disentangle myself from the exploitation and at twenty left this sham of treatment. I finished college and returned to the high school I had been attending when my father died, now as a young school teacher. Seeing my younger self reflected in so many of my students' faces, young students the same age as I was when I lost my father, I began to let myself see the vulnerability inherent to that age. I found my resolve to turn and take a stand against the exploitation, and called an attorney.

After the first news story of the lawsuit, more than twenty women spoke to my attorneys about their similar experience, with the same psychologist. Only three of us would engage a class-action lawsuit. Many feared societal repercussions and damage to their marriages. There were serious risks for the three of us who did undertake it: I feared losing my employment as a high school teacher. (What parent would want their children taught by a young woman who takes such a complaint public? This was the late 1970s; it just wasn't done.) There was deep apprehension that the trial would take place in a neighboring town that had not that long before removed signs reading "Whites only" from their public water fountains. Would a single, sexually active woman claiming harm from sexual exploitation find an understanding jury there? Doubtful. Perhaps worst of all, I felt such guilt for what this would ask of my family: to confront fear of scandal, to maneuver unnecessary embarrassment and to disavow undeserved shame. But my worst fears—unfounded—were that my family would turn away from me. They never wavered. Throughout it all, they kindled a small light—a light that might help Persephone in the darkness. They never questioned my resolve that I needed to give voice to biases that condemned women for sexual passions, shamed them for speaking out against abuse, shunned them for requiring respect.

We three plaintiffs, with two stalwart attorneys representing us, were eventually able to stop him, and in the years following, I learned what it meant to speak out against sexual exploitation, to bring forward complaints to the psychology licensing board in order to have him stripped of his license to practice. In those years and the years that followed, I learned to speak to power and to speak against prejudice towards women. It required some years in litigation; meetings with attorneys, undergoing depositions in which my complete sexual life and my partners were documented, to build the case against my assertion of damage, a case that "such a woman could not be damaged."

Yet unexpected, good things emerged from this horror. Had it not been for a canceled deposition in March of 1979—one for which I had prepared, one for which I had gathered my courage—I would not have been angry and distressed as I drove home. I would not have overreacted when a car I had not seen began to run a stop sign. I would not have swerved so violently to miss it that I lost control of my car, totaling it as I hit a curb, the wheels buckling on impact. I would not have walked to an office across the street and shakily called the police. I would not have met the officer who responded to the call, the man I would marry three years later, and to whom I am married still.

I would not have developed an interest in professional ethics, would not have taught them. I would not have stressed them in workshops and lectures. And, as a young psychologist in 1995, on behalf of the Texas Psychological Association, I would not have testified at the Texas legislature, urging the passage of Senator Judith Zaffirini's bill making sexual exploitation of patients a felony in the state. (They did. It is. For my part in this, you're welcome.)

While in the underworld, Persephone is said to have learned, to have grown into herself. Perhaps knowing that a loving other is searching for her, searching for a way to free her from her desolation, helped Persephone work on her side of things, to be ready to emerge when the way was found. I was well aware my family was searching for me, and that I was searching for myself. During the years of litigation, I returned to therapy, this time to work with a woman who guided me to greater understanding, greater self-respect, whose work with me leveled my inordinate guilt and began to soften my pain. She also reunited me with my dream: that I had wanted to study to be a psychologist, a dream dreamt when I was twelve and undreamt with the exploitation. I was most at home when learning, most at home when studying. It was then that the archetype of the wounded healer worked its way into my life.

*****

April 11, 1959
Dear Son,
Education teaches on how to be. Not how to be something, but how to be, how you live within your own mind. So, study hard son, and study all the things you think you may not need, the courses in literature and history and language and arts. Actually, they are the most important. They will make the You, the You

who must work and make a living, they will make the You more of a person, richer in thought, richer in capacity to live, abler to distinguish and appreciate what is good, and true, and beautiful.

As always, our love to you,
Dad

Graduate school called. I continued, with the help of my husband, to keep growing into myself, leaning on his compassion until I harnessed greater self-compassion than was my wont. Perhaps my greatest act of self-compassion was, upon starting my private practice, to enter a Jungian analysis. I was needing to wake up to myself, needing to understand what authority—what *female* authority—meant for my life. I was frustrated with anxiety, and beneath it all, aware that I was still hounded by unprocessed, orphaned grief, which needed to be brought home. My mother, in one of her most loving and wise interventions (and there were many), suggested I begin to read my father's letters. She wondered if *my* adult mind needed to know better *his* adult mind, to better understand the man who left too soon, to allow for a grief that could embrace his acceptance of his fate, and to stop holding myself so irrationally responsible for it all, none of which I could do if I kept seeing him only through the eyes of the child. She intuited, I fully believe, that if I could better know the mind of the man I grieved, I could return to Hades and bring Persephone back home.

*****

There is a thing about children leaving home, that they cannot come back. That is, they cannot come back and be the child they were before they left.

Neal Craig, July 18, 1970

*****

Emergence

I wonder, what did Persephone feel when she returned to the upper levels of the earth? Did she rejoice as her feet felt the grass beneath them? Did she feel herself inspired as she drank in fresh air, saw the dust motes dancing in rays of sunlight? A child no longer, did she set about to learn what she could, to prepare herself for the cycles of descent and emergence that come with living a conscious life? How does one find such grounding?

I took my mother's sage advice and turned to the letters. The treasures I have uncovered are many—there are thousands of pages. I began to understand the source of that inchoate knowing I had as a child, that knowing that I was never alone, that knowing that had been lost to me in Persephone's descent, that I was beginning to know again: page after page describing how both parents recognized their children's minds, what they saw of our unique characters, what they conveyed of our inherent worth. They were disciplinarians, often bemused and sometimes anguished by their need to be so, and they were each our biggest fans, not of our accomplishments, but of our wonderings, our questionings, our explorations. They thought of life as a pilgrimage, and along its way they required respect, gave respect, and nurtured insight.

During my analysis, I went on my own pilgrimage, taking a six-day silent retreat at the Lebh Shomea House of Prayer, a contemplative-eremitical community at La Parra Ranch, in Sarita, Texas. While Lebh Shomea does not promote itself as a wildlife sanctuary, it serves as an informal sanctuary to countless creatures. During my daily walks there, I witnessed nature's expressions of unseen presence. Though I did not see the animals, I saw evidence of them, not unlike witnessing the derivatives of complexes rather than the complex itself: turkey tracks here, the feather of a redtail hawk there. Perhaps there is no greater testament to the productive nature of regressive libido than the laborious accomplishment of the ever-backward-moving dung beetle. But the most striking evidence of an unseen presence was the savagely crushed branches beneath dense stands of oak and palmetto, where herds of wild javelina nest. The branches are not simply pressed down; they are *trodden* with such determined chthonic intention that one knows one is in the presence of a nature unapologetic of itself. At the core of the ego complex, the archetypal material of the Self takes a similar, chthonically unapologetic stance: "I Am that I Am," with no apologies, no explanations (*King James Bible*, 1769/2017, Ex. 3:14). It would be known at great cost to the ego and calls the ego on a pilgrimage that would bring that organ of consciousness into closer and fuller awareness of it.

The journey proved to be a paradox: to travel to a hermitage where one lives with intentional silence in hope of finding a way to speak about the act of pilgrimage, how it reflects an interior journey toward self-awareness. In the solitude of Lebh Shomea, silent meal after silent meal, day after day, I came to ponder how a conscious mind takes in an unseen presence, an unthought known. It is not only the presence of an abiding love—from both parents, for one another, for their children—it is how they bore witness of their children: to themselves, to those children, to the people they saw them becoming. At the heart of my pilgrimage, I found the dyad of silence and listening, reflected in 1 Kings 3:9: Give your servant *lebh shomea*—a listening heart—that I may be able to discern.

Upon my return, I poured over my parents' letters with a listening heart. Letters read in silence, letters laughed over with my mother and siblings, letters wept over in moments of sorrow. Letters of courtship, letters written long before any children were born, letters conveying the giving and receiving of support, of anxiety about the well-being of loved ones. In reading these letters, a minuscule few of which I have shared here, I reached back in time to ask my father the questions I had not known how to ask during my too-brief time with him. And he answered. In page after page, he reminded me that we cannot afford the luxury of ruminating on what might have been but are challenged throughout our lives to address what meets us. I have come to think of individuation not only as freeing myself from the grip of my complexes—of which I seem to have as many as the next person—but as growing into myself as fully and richly as I possibly can. It was never his intention, but my father taught me at so early an age that life was finite, that "our bodies were like clothes that we someday outgrow and cast off," and, in knowing this, to accept the obligation to live life fully. I was so lost in college, so very lost from my family and from myself. But no one is meant to wander in the desert forever, only for the time it takes to know that desolation is not the final stop, that desolation will crimp and constrain a person as much as any fundamentalism-born bias against women will. I return—both in reading the letters of my ancestors and to my own memory—to the abiding love that withstands the errors, the wrong turns, the misguided choices, and the moments of shadow possession so severe that one does not, at times, remember who one is.

I have, over the course of my life, found my way to my own voice, well aware of the refrains of my father's and mother's voices within my own. Finding one's voice does, I believe, walk hand in hand with finding one's authority. But in what does one's own authority lie? Experience perhaps, a willingness to question, to face uncertainties, to not believe the lie of desolation, that one is alone. I do know something of what might have happened had he lived. He would have used that extra time to foster my own authority in my life, to trust better my own sense of direction, to hold faster to my friends in times of need.

*****

February 7, 1970
Dearest Mother and Dad
There are a great many things that go through my mind these days. I am in a strange situation. I have one hand on the past, the time of your own youth, and of granddaddy's days, the dawn and rise of a new country with its frontiers and great expectations, its close tie to the earth of which we are part and are born. I suppose every man has a dream, and when he gets money enough, he builds an embellished cave to try to realize the dream. I have put many a dream on paper. But how remarkable that better dreams have so often come true, sometimes without our really dreaming them at all. I look at my wife and my children, and now at the work I am doing, and know how true that is.
Our children have been a joy to me. I could not say that one of them has been more of a joy than another. Each produced his problems, and all made the fine things that are within him. They have produced their own share of frets and anxieties for us, and the great wealth of the joy of their own mind and heart and love. We love you, and no day goes by in which we do not speak of you and think of you and talk of what you are and what you have done.

With all our heart's love,
Neal & Virginia

*****

In the hours before my father's death, my mother, brothers, sister and I—at my father's wish—took turns pressing on his chest so that he could breathe, as we waited for our eldest brother to arrive. Soon after he arrived, I asked my father if he wanted me to continue. He blinked once, for "no." I asked him if he wanted me to stop. He blinked twice, for "yes." Before I stopped—to go and fetch my family, to tell them it was time, to hear my brother Richard say, "I'm so sorry it was you he said this to"—I thought, "*I have so many questions, so very many questions that I don't know yet how to ask. I don't know what they are. I just know I have them.*" And with that thought, I stopped the compressions and went to my family, where they had taken some moments to rest. I looked about at what seemed a myriad of people who had gathered at our home. There, my father's beloved friend, Lyons, his fellow elder from our church back in Laredo. There, the woman ready to become my godmother if called, Camille. Both had rushed to Austin that morning—Lyons from Laredo, 245 miles to the south, Camille from Weatherford, 215 miles to the north—after each had dreamt the night before that they "needed to get to Neal."

I stopped, took a deep breath, and called my mother and siblings to come back to the bedroom.

*****

I have so many questions....
Carolyn, 1971–present

So, for my father, I have one last question, or perhaps, one last question for right now: Dad, what informed you, throughout your life, what informed your authority, your choices? What sustained you through the loss *you* had to contend with when such a debilitating disease would have you leave too soon?

> *There is perhaps no topic on which most of us are foggier than that of love; the most talked about, the most untaught. Perhaps most people see the problem of love primarily as that of <u>being loved</u>, rather than of*

loving. How do we regard it? Is it a skill, or an art? Does it require knowledge and effort? Is it a pleasant sensation which comes by fortuitous chance, something we fall into if we're lucky? People are starved for love. Babies have it. Teenagers cry for it. Adults work for it. The aged plead for it. The attitude that nothing is easier than to love continues to be prevalent in spite of overwhelming evidence to the contrary. But love is an art, a skill, a function to be learned. And despite the deep craving for love—to be loved—almost everything in Western Culture is considered more important: success, prestige, money, power. Love, devotion, is not a light word, and not an easy one.

Neal Craig, August 6, 1967
Notes on his sermon
"The Great Unknown"

I Still Listen for Her Voice

Nancy Qualls-Corbett

The collective unconscious—so far as we can say anything about it at all—appears to consist of mythological motifs or primordial images, for which reason the myths of all nations are its real exponents. In fact, the whole of mythology could be taken as a sort of projection of the collective unconscious. (Jung, 1954/1969, para. 325)

Extraordinary yet small occurrences happen to us all when seemingly our inner life expresses itself to consciousness. It may not be something earthshaking or flashy, but it does result in a dynamic life-changing experience. It's as if some bright spirit within wants to be recognized by ego-consciousness, to be lived out and find expression. Such an occasion occurred to me, although unknown at the time, when I came to find the symbol of the sacred prostitute, not only the writing of my book, but the complete revisioning of what the feminine archetype was really about and how it altered so much of how I experienced, understood, and loved my own feminine nature.

This occurred to me when I was studying at the Jung Institute in Zürich. It was the time in my training process to take the propaedeuticum, or the intermediate exam as it is now known. This is a test occurring midway through training which is a series of eight oral examinations, each test covering aspects of analytical training. The particular test I was preparing for was one relating to religion and psychology, where the candidate had to choose a particular symbol and trace it through a religious structure and also relate it to Jung's analytical teachings. We were to write a paper on our thoughts and findings and present it to our three examiners to be discussed with them. Prior to the exam the several candidates were to have a meeting with one of the examiners, present our chosen symbol, and he/she would then direct us in areas to research our topic. I couldn't decide on a symbol to declare and worried that perhaps it wasn't time for me to be tested. Perhaps I was rushing things. I decided to go to the meeting just to get some idea of what to expect. While walking there, I decided to just say I was not ready to declare my symbol, and ask, "May I be in touch at a later date?" Then, as it turned out, the other candidates and I were sitting in a circle talking and listening to the analyst who would be one of the examiners. He was asking each one of us what our symbol would be and then informing us of particular areas to study. One person said he chose the symbol of the well, another said she chose the symbol of a tree, and then it was my turn. I opened my mouth to say I wasn't prepared to state a symbol, but instead I said very clearly, "I choose the symbol of the sacred prostitute." I could hardly believe it! Those were my words, but *who* had said them? I was so stunned that I barely remembered the discussion afterward. It was as if an inner voice had chosen my symbol for me. Yes, I was aware through my readings of ancient religions that there were sacred prostitutes, the sensual priestesses of the goddesses of love—Aphrodite, Venus, Astarte, or Isis—and their ritual in the temple of love. However, I was quite unaware of that repressed image, her energy and dynamics and the real personification of the feminine within me. The sacred prostitute was the personification and advocate of the goddess of love.

I did prepare my paper after researching more completely about the actual ritual of sacred prostitution. The man, usually wanting sexual excitement, would come to the temple of the goddess of love and the human woman, a priestess of the goddess, would meet him, usher him into a chapel, and kneel with him before an image of the goddess: Together, they offered their prayers of devotion. Then they would enact this devotion with sexual intercourse. The act of experiencing love was transmitted one to another. This was like an initiation, a ritual for the man, of engendering more than physical pleasure; it also engendered soul, the feminine archetype. Although the physical reality seems identical, "having sex" and "making love" (literally) are opposite from one another. "Having sex" delights and feeds the personal ego and libido while "making love" feeds the soul and adds to the deepening of feelings of the other and the expansion of one's self for both partners. That is the true essence of the feminine archetype as described by Ann Ulanov in *The Feminine in Jungian Psychology and in Christian Theology*:

> *This highest phase of confrontation and individuation in both sexes is initiated by the feminine: for the man, through the anima, which leads to the self; for the woman, through the feminine self, not through any contrasexual elements. The feminine, in this sense, is the completing element; it is the feminine which completes the individuation of each sex. The masculine initiates the emergence of consciousness from primary unconsciousness; the feminine initiates the completion*

> *of consciousness by re-establishing contact with the unconscious. (p. 269)*

These were a few of the thoughts and ideas explored in the examination, which were approved, and I passed. When I was leaving the room, one of the examiners said, "I think you have a thesis topic there." I thanked her, but dismissed the idea as I went out the door. Then a year or so later, drawing near the time of finishing the program, I was in need of a thesis topic for the final examinations. No salient ideas would come … except words from the past: the sacred prostitute. Her image was still alive and active, and it felt as if she wouldn't let me go. It was as if she guided me through not only the historical, intellectual, and emotional paths of her own reality but also to a deeper level of my own emotional and psychological understanding of her reality. She was my final thesis topic.

This feeling, a mysterious sense of joy or peace, continued when I went into private practice as a Jungian psychoanalyst. I could see in patients' dreams elements of the abused or negated feminine principle and the resulting troubling complexes. There were dreams from both men and women of abused feminine figures of all ages, and some dreams in which young girls were sexually assaulted or women were slaves. In these dreams, the development of the feminine was surrounded by a negative complex that disallowed new conscious awareness of this archetype.

I was never a writer, nor thought to be one, but someone suggested working the thesis topic into a book. Once again her spirit was enlivened and "she" demanded to be heard. Thus, "we," that archetypal image and energy and I, wrote the book *The Sacred Prostitute: Eternal Aspect of the Feminine*.

It was through this inner counsel and advice that I truly came to know what the meaning of the feminine was, not just another term for "woman" or "the female sex," but the exploration of one's deeper, soulful life when made conscious. I was very restricted in my understanding of this, in part due to the time and environment in which I was raised and also the parental background that affected my sense of self. I was raised in the 1930s and early 1940s in a Southern small town which had a very conventional collective ethos. Women were good wives and mothers, providing good meals on the tables, sewing and knitting garments for their children, enjoying tea parties and weekly bridge games with women friends, and being active members of a church community. These were the attitudes that defined the feminine role, or that of a woman. And yes, for the most part, it did provide a sense of peace and harmony in the home and community, but for the wife or mother herself, it was a role she consciously enacted, a persona. There was certainly something deep in the unconscious that was yet to be known by ego consciousness.

My role model was my mother and certainly her ancestral line. She was born and raised in Italy, which encompassed a strong Roman Catholic faith, although after moving to America as a teen-ager and in later years marrying my American father, she did become Protestant. Her religious beliefs remained, as did her rosary beads, in the top drawer of her dresser. If attachment to this keepsake was of ancestry remembrance or religious faith, or both, I had no idea. My mother never taught my sisters or me about our sexual body or emotions. If anything, sexual intercourse was considered simply a wifely duty and the procedure for having children.

My father was the one who planted the seed of the more soulful aspect of our expressions of love, although it has taken me a lifetime to realize this. My bedtime stories were not the usual children's "Hansel and Gretel" or "Cinderella." My father read to me Greek and Roman mythologies, and I found them most exciting, especially those about the goddesses. In my small-town Southern Protestant environment, I had never heard about goddesses; only One God the Father. Naturally, I was also confused. If ancient religions could have goddesses, why couldn't we in this day and time? One day when I was about eight or ten years of age, I approached our pastor with this question. I think he must have been somewhat shocked, but he calmly answered something to the effect of, "Well, things have certainly changed since our ancient times, and we have grown in our knowledge and understanding. Certainly, women were important in ancient times, as they are today, but we also have to acknowledge the fact that it is your father's name that you carry, the man's name to identify who you are. It is the same with God the Father, whom we identify with, whose name we carry." I recall still being confused: I wanted to believe in the pastor's station, his knowledge, but I still longed for the essence and enlightenment of Venus or Aphrodite.

My life continued, a growing teenager with the images of the feminine taking shape as a sexy, emotional woman as seen in the moving pictures, simply more persona and ego-enhancing. This feminine image did not reach the fuller depth of soulful relationships, one of inner responsiveness that the goddess of love symbolized. However, the emotional enactment of falling in love occurred while I was in nursing school. I met a medical student, and we were married some months later after we both had graduated. This did awaken my soul. I deeply loved and cared for the other. It was as if we had both knelt down before the Goddess of Love and received her blessing. We parented three loving children and later parented foster twin boys. Certainly, the wife-mother role was hard at work, but there was something new. It was the family closeness, the caring, the experiencing of the true feelings of the others, both good and sad, evoking in me a true joy of others. I slowly realized this new awakening was the archetype of the feminine that prevailed throughout our relatedness. This isn't to say there were not rough times of disagreements or remarks meant to hurt or demean. But the basic attribute was there to approach these critical times by understanding the other's feelings and reaching out to them.

When our children were all in college, my husband and I made the choice to completely change our lives, so well known now as Jung's description of "the second half of life." I recall the moment well. One evening while preparing dinner for two after always feeding a large family, I laughingly remarked, "I don't have a pot small enough to cook for two. What is that saying about the rest of our lives?" Looking very serious and without a pause, he said, "Move to Zürich." We had been in a group "Centerpoint" studying the works of Carl Jung and pursuing individual analysis with a Jungian analyst. What a change of life! My husband resigned from his private medical practice, his position in the community, and I resigned from my prominent housewife and mother roles, my active community volunteer work, our social affairs hostess and coordinator, etc.

And, so, we began a new life. We both became students at The C. G. Jung Institute Zürich in the study of psychoanalysis. The old collective roles and personas disappeared. More than just a marriage partnership, we were also colleagues. And without that old persona identification of "woman's role," a new sense of myself began to develop, a sense of expanded purpose in my own life—not one defined by my conventional roles. Again, the feminine archetype continued to develop. It began to recognize the masculine archetype, the animus within, as well, consciously acknowledging and inviting this energy of intellect, purpose, discernment. It was indeed a special union, the "hierosgamos" or sacred marriage. Jung describes the hierosgamos as the psychic process which brings about the "'earthing' of the spirit and the spiritualizing of the earth, the union of opposites and reconciliation of the divided" (Jung, 1955–56/1970, para. 207).

Certainly, throughout the decades the life of a woman is no longer caught in the same collective roles as my early life taught me. We seem to be in a transitional time moving from extreme patriarchy to matriarchy. In some undeveloped countries, women can now be educated, have driver's licenses, and there are laws against removing a girl's clitoris. Much has changed in our country as well, as women are now educated and very capable of carrying out very important professions and making extraordinary contributions in what was once thought to be only a man's professional category: medicine, law, science, religion, and politics, to name only a few. But what has happened to the deep-seated feminine archetype, that one archetype which can make us more conscious of the real essence of our soulful love, the archetype that unites, is relational, feels compassion, benefits the weary or abused in truly caring for others? She does not seem to be that prevalent in modern-day society. Yes, sexual activities abound, but are they infused with soulful love or just enacted for physical and ego excitement? Does the higher level of matriarchy today, i.e., women's professional status equaling that of men's, carry the true essence of the feminine, or does it just mimic the same type of testosterone reaction (that is, I am the man, the boss, the one in charge here) although in a different body type?

One of the most depressive scenes I frequently see is a family seated at a restaurant table, and each member is engaged with his or her individual smart phone. There is no interaction, no conversation for fun or joy. I wonder how the individual egos must feel completely alone, unseen, unvalued. Psychologists are now speaking and writing on the "Loneliness Epidemic," and such scenes as described above are certainly symptomatic of it. And this lonely feeling grows to erupt in our culture with outbreaks of violence to others, like shootings in schools, churches, synagogues, or other public places, or in private spaces as physical abuse, rape, or slander. The basic cause of violence is the loss of the feminine archetype, of being valued, seen, loved for one's own being, which then escalates into destructive conflicts and wars where innocent people are left without a life, maybe literally. Certainly, the one they once knew is completely destroyed.

The feminine archetype is not to be thought of as weak; quite the opposite. Unlike our idealization of physical strength, it exemplifies an inner strength. It is an archetypal image of Eros, a tremendous basic strength which unites and enables the sacred marriage in life. It is an internal psychological process uniting the opposites of which our body and soul are composed: consciousness and unconsciousness, masculine and feminine, spirit and matter (body), intellect and wisdom. All within us that is divided or not in harmony disallows the fullness of experiencing one's unique Self, with a capital S. The Self, as Jung describes it, is the archetype of wholeness. It holds the master plan, as it were, the potentiality that enables us to realize the very person we were created to be.

When reviewing my story, I am so aware of how my life (now at age 93) has been so enlightened by the degrees of emergence into consciousness of the feminine archetype and how this feminine archetype, personified by me as the sacred prostitute, has initiated, awakened, surprised, and brought about a more complete feeling of my sense of Self. And although I hear very poorly in the outer world, I continue to listen to that inner voice to guide me once again, to lead me to the next experience or realization.

A Love Story

Susan Clements Negley

Part 1

Free Love

The 1960s ushered in a new era for women and our sexuality. We were young girls untutored by 1950s mothers who had not known their own sexual freedom. The birth control pill sometimes protected us from pregnancy, but not from venereal disease nor exploitation. The lucky girls experimented with their hippie boyfriends, but for me it was a free-for-all that tapped into childhood abandonment and a search for love.

While *Our Body, Ourselves* conferences were being held on the East coast, nothing of the sort had permeated as far down as south Texas. Lovability was measured in head counts, and other girls, like me, gave ourselves and our bodies away. Decades later, as a mother of three children, the youngest being a daughter, I was determined to do better than my mother had with me.

My daughter was turning sixteen when I decided to have "the talk." "You need to know that sometimes when a boy says he loves you, he just wants to have sex." To which she replied, "Who doesn't know that?"

I didn't, not until my forties. Bemoaning my relationship history with a trusted male colleague in my graduate program, I asked, "What does a man think when a woman takes her clothes off for him?" I was thinking that for sure he knows she is looking for relationship and love. "That she wants to have sex?" he said.

That afternoon was the beginning of an awakening. I was sadly reminded of all the mornings after, and of the days waiting by the phone, for a call that never came.

Constant Craving

I spent a good part of my adult life and years of analysis trying to understand my "father complex" and anaclitic depressions. The psychoanalytic text *Narration of Desire* (Wrye & Welles, 1998) turned the focus to the mother with whom we have our first exchange of fluids, an exchange of cells through the placenta where we literally become enmeshed, "flesh of my flesh" (Genesis 2:23). In my case the erotic connection to my mother's body was ripped away by my stepfather at the suspiciously Oedipal age of five years old. In gin-infused confessions, he proudly and defiantly claimed her as his own: "I didn't want more children; I wanted your mother." They traveled the world.

Time with my biological father, typically a daughter's first love, was relegated to the second weekend of every month and every other holiday. This led to a lonely childhood and a lifelong fear of abandonment. Both losses led to constant craving and promiscuity at a very early age.

What to do with all the secrets and shame? Women are inhibited in sharing our sexual secrets, in part to protect our children, and even partners, who might not have the stomach for the whore part of the Madonna/whore split.

I was one of the lucky ones. Through my analysis I found a tribe of professionals and seekers who had a shared belief that it was time for HER[1] to step back out onto the stage. After five thousand years of patriarchal domination, it was time for the return of "the feminine."

In her book *The Sacred Prostitute* (1988), Jungian analyst Nancy Qualls-Corbett offered us a new vision of ourselves awakening to some deep, dark mysterious feminine that redeemed, reframed, and reimagined our concept of our lusty selves. Maybe we hadn't been punished by Venus with disease, and our menses wasn't a curse after all.

Healing Comes Where We Least Expect It

A female analysand that I was treating for PTSD had been a chaplain in the Iraqi war. When she sent me this biblical passage from *Ezekiel 16,* I had no context for the narrative of this ancient verse, and Old Testament prophets were new to me. My patient had seen something relevant to her own personal experience, and, upon reading it, I found something relevant to mine.

> *16:4 At birth, the very day you were born, there was no one to cut your navel-string, or wash you in cleansing water, or rub you with salt, or wrap you in napkins.*
> *16:5 No one leaned kindly over you to do anything like that for you. You were exposed in the open fields; you were as unloved as on the day you were born.*
> *16:6 Abandoned at birth I found you there: Live, said the Lord,*

[1] Terms that are entirely capitalized refer to an archetypal pattern or the designation of an archetype.

16:7 and grow like the grass of the fields. You developed, you grew, it was time for your womanhood.
16:8 Then I passed by you and saw you, and behold, you were at the time for love; so I spread my skirt over you and covered your nakedness. I adorned you with ornaments, put bracelets on your hands and a necklace around your neck, earrings in your ears and a beautiful crown on your head. Thus you were adorned with gold and silver, I also swore to you and entered into a covenant with you so that you became Mine, declares the Lord.
16:17 But in your whoring you have taken my presents of gold and silver and made yourself human images.
16:19 The bread I gave you, the finest flour, oil and honey with which I used to feed you, you have now offered to them as an appeasing fragrance to others.
16:20 You have even—it is the Lord who speaks—taken the sons and daughters you bore me and sacrificed them.
16:30 How easily led you were—it is the Lord who speaks—you were not out for money: a prostitute is paid. But you have given your gifts away to all your lovers.
16:35 Well then hear the word of the Lord.
16:42 I will exhaust my fury against you. My jealousy will then leave you; I shall be appeased, and my anger will stop.
16:44 Now all the proverb-makers will make up a proverb about you: Like mother, like daughter.
16:45 Yes; you are a true daughter of your mother, who hated her husband and her children; a true sister

of your sisters, who hated their husbands and their children.
16:53 I will restore you and I will restore your sisters, that you may bear your shame and console them.
16:60 but I will remember the covenant that I made with you when you were a girl, and I will conclude a covenant with you that shall last forever.
16:61 And you for your part will remember your past behavior. I take your elder and younger sisters and make them your daughters, although this was not included in this covenant.
16:62 I am going to renew my covenant with you; and you will learn that I am the Lord.

We can be certain that the ancient priests, the Men of the Great Assembly, interpreted Ezekiel's vision to serve their own ends. I am also aware that in this analysis I have done the same. My first reading blew past the painfully patriarchal and misogynistic language of the translation and in so doing, I saw an aspect of my life story and a love story that was being revealed to me. I was tempted to exchange the word "whore" for "desperation," but it was the rawness of the text that held much of its power for me.

My Birth Story

My personal story and subsequent healing journey resonate within Ezekiel's passages.

16:4 At birth, the very day you were born, there was no one to cut your navel-string, or wash you in cleansing water, or rub you with salt, or wrap you in napkins.
16:5 No one leaned kindly over you to do anything like that for you. You were exposed in the open fields; you were as unloved as on the day you were born.

My mother told me of turning away from the bundle she was being offered by the attending nurse at my birth. Her pregnancy was unplanned, and she had been forced into a shotgun marriage by angry parents.

My analysand saw her young self—abandoned in the field, uncared for and un-caressed, and I too had been denied my own mother's loving touch. We were both left in the open *psychic* field, the matrix of the unconscious, unmediated by the soothing, containing embrace of the nourishing biological mother.

Jung said that an archetypal problem requires an archetypal solution, but when we are helpless and weak, "the helpful powers slumbering in the deeper strata of man's nature can come awake and intervene" (1954/1969, para. 44).

> *16.6 and 16.7 Abandoned at birth I found you there: Live, said the Lord, and grow like the grass of the fields. You developed, you grew, it was time for your womanhood.*

Nature takes her course. The need for attachment never lessens, but we are designed as highly adaptive beings with a myriad of strategies and coping styles. Despite rejection and neglect, the powerful instinct for life finds nourishment, which increases our chance for survival. The religious instinct in the psyche mobilizes the deepest layers of the unconscious and the inner mystery of spiritual awakenings. In this dual container, a vessel created from psyche and matter, we are cocooned for transformation.

> *16:8 Then I passed by you and saw you, and behold, you were at the time for love; so I spread my skirt over you and covered your nakedness.*

In the many readings of this verse over the years (and I still shed tears every time), the "I" in the narrative initially felt like an overwhelmingly powerful but protective masculine figure who claimed and loved me, while also calling me out, and up, to a higher consciousness. It took several years and many more readings before I recognized a feminine presence. She slipped in, "I passed by you and covered you with my skirt." The divine feminine is often hidden, especially within the Christian tradition. While HE demanded that I take charge of my life, SHE ushered in something different. In this passage SHE appears as a powerful protective intercessor.

The archetypal feminine comes in when the biological mother cannot. An example of this came in a dream during a difficult time of self-doubt:

> *A very old African American woman cups my face in her hands and says to my much younger and smaller self, "Susie, you are the cream of the cream of the crop."*

This earthy woman communicated warmth and unconditional affirming love. I felt cared about and blessed by this ancient woman; my child-self felt special and seen, while my adult-self felt the acknowledgment of my individuality. An irony lies within. When my mother and stepfather would return from their travels, my stepfather would describe the wealthy, powerful people they traveled the world with as the "crème de la crème." In this dream the ancient and wise woman confers on young Susie a blessing of *her* value, as if in response to the power of my stepfather's words on the ears of a little child.

Blessings

> *16.9 I adorned you with ornaments, put bracelets on your hands and a necklace around your neck, earrings in your ears and a beautiful crown on your head. Thus you were adorned with gold and silver, I also swore to*

> *you and entered into a covenant with you so that you became Mine, declares the Lord.*

Girls are initiated into womanhood through their first blood. Nature endows us with gifts (resources physical and spiritual), which are the *prima materia* for future development. When young girls want to dress up and wear crowns and tiaras, parents cluck at the "Little Princess," sometimes missing her precognition as Queen, as does the woman/child who clings to her youth. Early dreams of weddings, gold rings, and silver goblets are a first hint, an innate precognition of the *hierosgamos,* a sacred marriage representing our potential wholeness. Gold and silver are the noble substances representing sun and moon, masculine and feminine dimensions, uniting the opposites in this holy marriage.

Crowning, the symbolic opening of the crown *chakra*, the term used when the top of the baby's head comes through the mother's vagina, represents a second birth into the next cycle of a young woman's life. This psychic birth is out of the womb of childhood and rebirth into a new self-image. Yet there was no biblical "red tent" in our 1960s Western culture, no sacred space for girls and women to find support and encouragement from each other. No rite of initiation into the profound mysteries of womanhood. No celebration. Blood, evidence of our curse.

Our bodies, fertile and fecund, drew us into a blend of darkness and innocence. When I was thirteen years old, I had a dream of a boy, my age, coming naked through a stark and rugged canyon, erotic but not yet sexual. It was an introduction to something new that held a promise. When our young bodies woke up to new sensations, our desire felt like a delicious but dangerous secret. Sending a message of unacceptability, our parents sent us upstairs in our miniskirts and crop tops to "go cover ourselves."

> *16:17 But in your whoring you have taken my presents of gold and silver and made yourself human images.*

Misguided by an overly sexualized culture, we projected all our goods—our gold—onto boys and men. We went "boy crazy" and worshipped them as idols. Projecting our self-worth onto others left us feeling empty and worthless when they left us behind.

In Western culture the dominant myth for many women could be captured in the fairy tale cliché, "My prince will come." My mother, a beautiful Aphrodite woman of her time and upbringing, was described to me by a stranger as "the woman of every man's dreams." Even though I consciously rejected and despised my mother's way of life, I identified with her attractiveness to men in my unconscious, "like mother, like daughter." On her deathbed my wasting mother was encouraged to eat to keep her strength a little longer. Referring to her third husband, she objected "but he likes thin." Her deeply ingrained instinct for life, attaching to powerful men, finally became an instinct for death, as she lay there dying, thin indeed.

> *16:30 How easily led you were—it is the Lord who speaks—you were not out for money: a prostitute is paid. But you have given your gifts away to all your lovers.*

Women who had sex before marriage were accused of giving "our milk" away for free. Wasn't the "for free" of this criticism implying that we should be paid, and isn't this a type of grooming for socially acceptable prostitution?

When I confessed an erotic transference early in treatment with a male analyst, he responded, "You're too easy." This felt true—along with a familiar shaming—but I was again misunderstood. My sharing was inspired in a session by a flood of feeling, the same feeling I had on the edge of my pubescence when the boy came through the canyon. Erotic but not yet sexual and very, very young. "You're too easy" was a message I didn't understand but, nonetheless, it shut the feelings down, a truly lost moment.

As with my patient, early abandonment left us desperate for connection. Out of a missing sense of self, I had no respect for self, no concept of self-respect. Despite a fierce rebellion and independence, witnessing my father's and stepfather's physical and verbal abuse of my mother left a blind spot in my psyche. Subsequently, I did not experience my body as my own. I now understand my mother's submission as survival and even ambition. She wanted to be a "somebody," and this was the only way she knew how. At what cost?

> *16:20 You have even—it is the Lord who speaks—taken the sons and daughters you bore me and sacrificed them.*

And at times, yes, like my mother, I abandoned my own children when in hot pursuit of a new romance or became emotionally unavailable when dealing with yet another heartbreak. This acknowledgment is the most painful of all. Yes, like mother, like daughter.

> *16:45 Yes; you are a true daughter of your mother, who hated her husband and her children; a true sister of your sisters, who hated their husbands and their children.*

In my family the beautiful Queen was my mother. I still remember where my twelve-year-old self was standing when my mother said, "You are getting very pretty." It felt dark, like a hiss, as if I had done something wrong. I was confused. Having been a chubby, depressed, and angry child, I surely didn't feel pretty. The "blessing" time for a young girl's transition to womanhood in my case felt more like a warning or a curse. My mother didn't hate me;

it was a comment born out of a deeply ingrained desperation from having no real power for women of her status and culture.

Later in my adolescence I was confused but also frightened when my stepfather said there was a competition between my mother and me. I had no sense of this, nor could I understand a world where a girl would be competing with her "mommy" for anything. I only realized later in life that "being the fairest in the land" offered my mother a life she couldn't conceive of having without being attached to powerful men. She had been abused and was a survivor too.

When it was time to marry, I unconsciously chose the man of my mother's dreams, powerful and wealthy, and unavailable for intimate love. In my family and community, men were the prize. Women elders, mothers and mothers-in-law, counseled women against each other. "There's one hiding behind every bush." The message was that women were vying for the available resources, and, if you weren't careful, or didn't play your cards right, it could be your husband that they took. Women weren't to be trusted, so we didn't trust ourselves. Self-love turned to self-hatred, internalized misogyny.

My mother confessed once she didn't really like women, but later in her life, through her golf games, she made some close friends. I'm not sure how much she shared of herself, but I was glad for her. After her death, and in a late attempt to heal beyond the stuck narrative I was in, I invited one of those trusted friends to lunch. When I asked her how much of my story my mother had shared, my decision to leave my husband despite having three young children, she replied, "She was always protective of you." That day I realized that my mother, in her own way, had covered me with her skirt, *had* in her own way protected me. These many years after her death, I could feel a healing, an opening to our love.

> *16:19 The bread I gave you, the finest flour, oil and honey with which I used to feed you, you have now offered to them as an appeasing fragrance to others.*

And to convince the reader of the shocking correspondence to my own story that I saw in Ezekiel's prophecy, I had had a career as a professional cook. I took my hunger and need for nurturance and turned it outward into the feeding of other people. When I dream that I am back in the catering business, it is a high sign of too much service and caretaking. It's time to feed myself.

Return

> *16:60 but I will remember the covenant that I made with you when you were a girl, and I will conclude a covenant with you that shall last forever.*

Read through the lens of depth psychology, the Lord is understood as the god image within each of us, the central transcendent operating system at the core of the personality. I was estranged from myself, but a Self that was always there and waiting.

The real moment of epiphany came to me when I felt the "Otherness" of the Lord and the "never let you go-ness" of the love. While waiting at a stop light, I heard a voice: "I was there at the beginning."

While delving deeply into the Ezekiel text and experiencing its profound meaning for me, a word came into my consciousness. It is strange when a word like "defiled" becomes *numinous*. Etymologically speaking, it was me who had "trampled over and abused" myself. When I recognized that the who or what I had been estranged from and betrayed by was also me, a strangely paradoxical feeling came over me. It was free love: profound, private, unconditional, eternal. Yes, boys and men had hurt me, but *I had hurt myself* (because I was hurting). That I would no longer be an unconscious victim of "out there" was a strangely empowering and liberating feeling. Yes, patriarchy was and is brutal, but now guys in the world could be just guys—with their own stories of longing and desire. I had a new experience: self-respect, real treasure.

> *16:53 I will restore you and I will restore your sisters, that you may bear your shame and console them.*
> *16:61 And you for your part will remember your past behavior.*

Facing these facts, encountering the shadow side of the love story, has indeed informed my work with women in my analytic practice: mothers, daughters, and sisters offering consolation, articulation, and healing. I see a new generation of women emerging, and we have generations of women to guide us. I am filled with hope. Deep feminine knowledge is speaking to us if we will stop to listen.

> From the *Apocrypha, Wisdom 7:11*:
> *All good things came to me, and of her hands riches not to be numbered.*

The Great Mother or goddess archetype dwells in the psyche of all women.

Part 2

During this extensive time of process and insight I found my true love. He introduced himself to me *in a dream* during a five-minute nap on an airline flight. I happened to be struggling with yet another love affair just having gone down in flames. He said his name *exactly* like this:

> *"I am THE INNER SECRET LOVER OR THE SECRET INNER LOVER."*[2**] *I didn't see this mysterious stranger, only the gift He offered: a box which, when opened, revealed a pair of emerald shoes.*

A few hours later I picked up a fashion magazine, and on the back cover was an image of a mysterious woman holding in front of her face, as an offering, a pair of brilliant emerald shoes. Some years prior this same brilliant green had appeared in another dream immediately following the death of a loved one. In that dream a holographic emerald tablet emerged as a symbol of the young woman's physical transformation and the creation of the diamond body, her true indestructible essence. The dream of the emerald tablet came at just the right time, a time of grief, as did the dream offering from the "INNER LOVER."

> Jung describes a "blessed greenness" or *benedicta viriditas* as:
> *...the state of someone who, in his wanderings among the mazes of his psychic transformation, comes upon a secret happiness which reconciles him to his apparent loneliness. In communing with himself he finds not deadly boredom and melancholy but an inner partner; more than that, a relationship that seems like the happiness of a secret love, or like a hidden springtime, when the green seed sprouts from the barren earth, holding out the promise of future harvests. (1955-56/1970, para. 623)*

---

[2] ** I came to understand the ambiguity in his name: THE INNER SECRET LOVER as the lover of inner secrets and the SECRET INNER LOVER as the inner beloved, spiritual animus, soul guide. Both aspects of his message to me can be found in the *benedicta viriditas* in the text. THE INNER SECRET LOVER OR THE SECRET INNER LOVER will henceforth be referred to as the INNER LOVER.

It signifies "on the one hand the 'leprosy of the metals' (verdigris), but on the other the secret immanence of the divine spirit of life in all things" (Jung, 1955-56/1970, para. 623).

Wearing the emerald shoes, I feel a little like Dorothy as she is wandering through the maze of her own psychic transformation. While her *ruby* shoes represent passion and commitment to the journey, another dream speaks to the demands of the "INNER LOVER" for a different kind of commitment. He wants a committed relationship, and the gift of the emerald shoes signifies a new standpoint.

In another dream:

> *The man at the bar hands me a piece of paper with his contact info and the words "Call me sometime to keep it real." He asks me if there is a man back home, and I say, "Yes. We are dating." He says, "We don't date."*

The previous scripture from *Ezekiel 16*, in its translations, has the feeling of the Old Testament God, jealous and punishing. This dream led me to a different experience. While my spiritual life and my understanding of many mysterious "truths" have come through a devoted practice to my dreams, this *direct* contact with the Lover and the feelings with which he engages me was new. I felt his intense interest in me, and with it the awareness that this exhilarating pleasure was going to cost me something. Sacrifice is a painful relinquishing of a fantasy.

First and foremost is the fantasy that *he* is out there, and therefore the necessity to stop looking. He was uncompromising.

My childhood obsession with the song "Can't Find My Way Home" written by Stevie Winwood captured the feeling of being lost but with an important message encoded in the lyrics:

Come down off your throne and leave your body alone
Somebody must change
You are the reason I've been waiting so long
Somebody holds the key. (Winwood, 1969)

While women are described by wishful-thinking men as basically monogamous, the polyamorous Self knows better. And while I understand this "We" in the "don't date" dream refers to the *various* forms of a woman's *animus*, I am intentionally referring to the Lover, who happens to be the "somebody" who holds the key. I want to stay close to the sensing body and this healing story of a lovesick child, the poetry of "some" "body," a hint of the movement towards the healing of the sensing self.

The Bridge

My understanding of the bridge between the carnal and spiritual aspects of love came in a series of dreams.

> *I am swimming laps in an Olympic pool shaped like a racetrack and am aware that, not far away, a man reclining on a white marble bench up on a hill is watching me. I am now transported into an enclosed space with him, and our encounter is sealed with a kiss. His name is Jeff Bridges.*

Perfect choice. According to Jung, when consciousness makes a commitment to constant contact with the unconscious, it is paying "a tribute that more or less guarantees its co-operation" (1955-56/1970, para. 40).

The psyche chooses not only an actor to whom I am attracted, but in its marvelous poetry, an actor whose name describes the function of the *animus* in women's unconscious. According to Jung, the *animus* "bridges" consciousness to the unconscious, and Jeff Bridges in the dream becomes the conduit for this relationship, which is sealed with a kiss. Jungian analyst Marilyn Marshall (2005), in her study of the various interpretations of the symbolism of the kiss, identifies one aspect of the kiss as an *unio mystica*, a union with the divine. "This kiss…unites the masculine and feminine in an outward portrayal of an inner potentiality that brings the unknown, contra-sexual Other, the anima/animus, into relationship with consciousness" (Marshall, 2005, p. 131). The kiss is the bridge between consciousness and the deepest layers of the unconscious, where we communicate with the divine.

> *16:62 I am going to renew my covenant with you; and you will learn that I am the Lord.*

According to Jung, it takes a partner in the world to arouse the "powerfully suggestive" archetypes (1951/1968, para. 34). Thinking this truer in a younger woman than those who are more psychologically mature, it was, in fact, a chance encounter with a previous lover that I will call John who kickstarted for me a wholly/holy new and deeper understanding of the living processes of the psyche through its *passion.* I was given an opportunity to understand that its *telos,* its aim for wholeness, must be experienced through the mind *and with the body.*

Wisdom and experience, fate and luck, guided this part of my journey.

Experience told me this fateful encounter was *not* about the man but the way he made me *feel.* I was lucky enough not to be available for a new relationship. This constellated a relational field that wouldn't be acted out. Consciousness dictated, "There's no way this is going to happen." This hermetically sealed container created a highly charged environment, and the intense physical desire seeded the unconscious, which produced a series of delicious dreams.

John and I enter a restaurant and, as I seat myself at a table, he pushes his chair away and offers me his hand. It is an invitation to dance. I tell him shyly that I can't dance, but he insists and pulls me to him. I step up on his feet and we place our foreheads together. We begin to sing a sweet song in perfect harmony.

In ceremony, sacred ritual, chanting, and dance open a space for the divine. Claimed by the powers of the unconscious, the sensual dance and song bridge the body and soul, the feeling of a powerful experience of union that for a moment extinguishes exquisitely painful longing. I feel lured by the unconscious further into the depths, with no idea yet where I am going. The alchemical psyche cooked up just the right love potion to leave me wanting more.

John, my partner in the dream dance, was many years in recovery, and I believe he represents sobriety and a relationship to a higher power. Sobriety is another example of containment, and for some the necessary condition for having an actual spiritual experience as opposed to the distracting "spirit" in the bottle. A dream expressed the accomplishment of this containment:

Holding up a clay vessel, John, the earthy artist, won first prize in the art show.

The relinquishing of addictions, distractions, and dalliances wins first prize, but holding and containing the spellcasting, intoxicating desire for the earthy/earthly man was deeply challenging. I decided that he represented my creative *animus*, so I tried to channel my creative juices into new artistic endeavors. I signed up for art classes, but to no avail. The more I tried to intellectualize my experience, the more my body resisted and insisted, demanding attention, not putting up with any mind-body splitting. Embodiment took on a whole new meaning, and further instruction came in another swimming pool dream:

> *From a bird's eye view, I see the naked female swimmer doing the breaststroke and frog kick in an Olympic-size swimming pool. John is standing up on a hill also watching her. I am at the same time the swimmer.*

What was I still to learn about the male gaze such that it appeared in yet another dream? The controversial radical feminist and art historian Camille Paglia, a biological reductionist, attributes the male gaze to the hunting archetype. My reference to a bird's eye view also sounds predatory. The feeling in the dream was beyond sexual instinct or desire. It was a highly charged field of energy, intoxicating, like a beautiful perfume that wafted through the air, evoking not lust, but love and admiration. I interpret this dream as an image of alchemical cooperation, copulation between the biological and the spiritual. The frog kick and the breaststroke were animating, arousing, and stimulating, the necessary energy to release the powerful elixir that permeated the field: Eros.

I came out one morning to find two beautiful green lizards mating outside my kitchen door. The female looked trapped in an alarmingly violent leglock. That very night I had a dream where I was being held by a strange man in the same embrace but, unlike my female lizard counterpart, I was trying desperately to squirm free. What is this resistance? Fear of male domination, of being trapped?

Theoretically, a lack of relation to the positive *animus* activates possession by the negative *animus.*

After entering active imagination, bathed in the feeling tone of the second swimming pool dream, my body softened into a mutual and loving embrace. I no longer felt captive. A subsequent dream of the same embrace reminded me of the comfort of entwined and interlocking legs. The feeling in this dream is beyond the undifferentiated merged state of oneness between a mother and child, but instead expresses the core alchemical belief that only separate substances can unite.

My "INNER LOVER" was guiding me. Holding the tension, struggling with desire seeking somewhere to go, my distant Puritan minister ancestor, Cotton Mather, breathing down my neck, I had a synchronistic experience. A fragment of a poem by Rumi was posted on Facebook by a stranger. Oh, the strange cracks where the light comes through, analysands, airplanes, social media:

Out beyond ideas of wrongdoing and rightdoing,
there is a field. I'll meet you there.

When the soul lies down in that grass,
the world is too full to talk about.
Ideas, language, even the phrase each other
doesn't make any sense. (Rūmī, 1995, p. 36)

This poem was followed by a dream:

I am walking alone down a country road. I am aware that up ahead and to my left there is a field of green grass. It is my destination, as if waiting for me.

Redemption

This is a Love Story and begins with a redemption song: the soul's struggle to restore its sovereignty. A fight for physical and mental freedom for women, for all of us who have struggled under an oppressive patriarchy. When we mature and choose to reveal ourselves, Wisdom brings discernment and insight and the fateful realization that we can protect ourselves and each other. Over time and through experience, our innocence is sacrificed for knowledge and understanding. This is an important part of any woman's love story as she moves into and stands in her own power.

Release from the conflict of right and wrong was an epiphany. Through a mystical experience in the land beyond words, I feel peace and connection.

I am alone but not alone, and my feelings of loneliness for a time disappear.

When some part of the psyche that we think is unknowable (our blind spot) is known, we get closer to the divine. So that's what it's about: God.

At the moment of my daughter's birth, the doctor turned towards her father and said, "Look, it's a girl. She's already got her hand out asking for something." My ears heard those words while the voice in my head heard this, "Who would have dared to hope." My daughter, presenting hands first through the birth canal, *is* asking for something. Divine Sophia is coming, too, and from somewhere deep within, we know this.

Eros and the Stranger

Janice Quinn

Called or uncalled, God is present!
(Jung, 1978, p. 164)

Eros Lost

When I was invited to write a chapter about Eros, I was thrilled! In an instant, I knew what I wanted to write about—Eros and the Stranger. My intent was to share a few short yet significant encounters of Eros and strangers that I have experienced in my life. It was as if Eros had struck me with one of his potent arrows, and I was very happy to feel his presence. But a strange thing happened as I began to focus on the writing; I was becoming estranged from Eros. It seemed like the more I tried to capture Him, the more He slipped away—as if *He* was becoming a *Stranger*.

I felt like Psyche, who raised a lighted candle in the dark to see her nightly lover, only to helplessly watch him fly away from her. Bereft and lackluster, I had no energy to write. But more than that, I had lost desire for anything whatsoever. Suddenly, everything became a daily slog. I could do nothing lightly, with a spring in my step. I told a friend I thought I was depressed. Yet even that did not feel like the right descriptor for this malaise. I sat paralyzed: blank in thought; blasé in feeling—a pure sense of nothingness.

I was descending into the very depths of my being—and I was lost. Truly a stranger in a strange land! My intent to describe the stranger had now pointed right at me, and I grasped for words to try to clothe my feeling of nakedness. Forced efforts met a blank page. Like Psyche sitting in utter despair and defeat, overwhelmed by the seemingly impossible challenges tasked by Aphrodite conditional to seeing Eros again, I felt a sense of complete hopelessness. I sat in the unknown, like Melancholia in Dürer's well-known woodcut image.

What happened? Where was Eros? Where was that lithe spirit? At the very apex of my life, why was I feeling so empty and depleted? Perhaps everything in the past few years was just now catching up with me, I thought. Was it the leftover effects of the pandemic, the horrors and forced shutdowns—physically and mentally—that we all had to face, as well as the millions of deaths worldwide that touched each of our lives? Was it the 2024 U.S. presidential election and the resulting fears of destabilization of our very sense of national identity and way of life? Was it a feeling that the number of wars were increasing with no end in sight—those bitter conflicts between people of differing cultures? Or was it more personal? Overall, I was feeling very good about my life, so this very dark, lonely place was confusing and disconcerting.

Usually, when I have felt in a quandary about something, a dream will emerge to help, like the ants who came to help Psyche sort the huge pile of seeds in Aphrodite's first task. But this time, there were no dreams, no help whatsoever from the unconscious realm or from the greater Self.

Psyche was intent on reuniting with Eros—as I was. It was necessary for her to complete the challenges and obstacles thrown to her by Aphrodite in order for her to truly see Eros again. Symbolically, this could be about working on the aspects of the unconscious that come up either through dreams or in analysis. So, like Psyche, I hunkered down and hoped to be reunited with Eros in a new, more integrated way of deeper connectedness and self-realization.

I then recalled I had been here before. It was at the beginning of my inner work many years ago. At that time, although I had achieved much success in life by outer standards, I became utterly estranged from myself and the world around me. As I sat in this existential crisis, I remembered the book *The Stranger* by Albert Camus (1989) in which he sees life as meaningless, even absurd. This sense of alienation causes us to grapple with the *stranger* within, and to realize that we are responsible for creating meaning as we make our own way in the world. Eros can cause chaos; He stirs us up, as does the stranger. Both draw us into other dimensions of life in the inner and outer worlds. Both can feel violent or like a rupture of our ordinary sense of things. When we are encountering the stranger, we become fearful, but also perhaps curious—unsure what will come. Is the stranger going to help us or hurt us? Can we survive the encounter? Will the experience be more constructive or destructive? We don't know. That is part of the mystery.

Eros and the Strange Land of Dreams

In my early thirties, when the inner world beckoned, I began to dream. This was in the first week of analysis and was a strange development in my life as I had not been aware of my dreams before this. I began to realize that these images were affecting me emotionally and transforming my perspectives on my life and life in general. These symbols were natural, high-powered energy forms that took me out of the familiar and routine and into another world within—that of the Unknown—a whole new strange world. Through my analytical process, there seemed to be *something* urging me on in this dark world. Eros was there offering greater understanding, empathy, and meaning to my life from the unconscious and, ultimately, from the Self.

Three dreams, in particular, stand out. In the first dream, a very old woman dressed in a tattered grey nun's habit had been hit by a passing car. She could not get up. She had a broken leg. When my analyst asked what I thought about this image, I said, "She looks like I feel." I was not aware at the time that I was suffering from a deep existential crisis of meaning. I just knew that I felt numb and that I had no desire to continue on with the life I was leading. I had eschewed therapy due to a strong religious upbringing in which both parents were trained church leaders, and my father's mantra was "All you need is the Bible." It had been especially difficult in our household to meet their expectations because they really did "walk the talk." In my efforts to find my own sense of self, I had striven mightily to live up to their standards.

From the perspective of the outer world, I looked very successful as an independent, self-assured professional woman. Armed with a master's degree in public administration from Harvard, I moved to Washington, D.C., where I began my career as a policy analyst for the U.S. Environmental Protection Agency. But after three years, I didn't feel like I was doing enough. I had some significant accomplishments, including several awards recognizing effective work in reducing and banning cancer-causing synthetic chemicals impacting the drinking water supplies. I was also involved in working with multiple government agencies and departments on a national plan for a multi-agency response to natural and manmade disasters, including acts of terrorism. I was in the highest echelons of the most powerful nation in the world, providing a great deal of effectiveness in environmental protection as well as the overall health of our nation and North America in general. I traveled extensively for work, connecting with officials on the Federal, State, and Local levels of government. As I handed in my resignation after eight years, my boss shockingly exclaimed,

"But you've made it!" I appreciated his recognition, but inside I felt devoid of life. Jung says where power dominates, love is absent. Although I felt I was doing very vital, enduring work for humankind, I did not feel the love.

I began to wonder how a woman acquires her individual identity and self-worth. Is it learned, passed down from generation to generation? Is it there at birth? Why do some women seem to move through horrible adversities and attain a sense of dignity and self-respect, when others feel embarrassed to be seen, while still others try to numb their pain with drugs, sex, alcohol, or food? Why do some develop psychological and/or physical disturbances, while others end their lives altogether? How do women gain a sense of self-worth, especially in a cultural milieu where men and male-oriented values have been and continue to be predominant? And what about men? If they have been taught to devalue the feminine aspects of their being and to devalue the women in their lives, how does this affect their sense of being and self-worth?

After the dream of the old woman, I had a second dream I called Mountain Woman. In this dream, I was hiking up a green, steep hill along a narrow dirt path and was getting tired. As I was about to turn back, a forest ranger dressed in a brown uniform came up over the ridge and motioned me upwards. With his encouragement, I continued to trudge upwards along the path. Upon reaching the top, I walked past two wooden coffins on either side of me that I suspected were holding my parents. I arrived at the top and looked out across the vast expanse. Across the way was a huge mountain that looked to have a stone woman carved in the face of it: She wore a long flowing robe and sat in a meditative state of inward contemplation. I realized I had two choices: I could hop in a nearby helicopter with its engine running and land on top of her, or I could go down the hill and ascend the rugged mountain, getting to know her every step of the way. I regarded the helicopter ride as the fast track I was on and the heady accomplishments already achieved. Doing things efficiently and expediently characterized my performance-oriented life. The climb would be an arduous journey, but I knew that was what I had to do to become more fully connected with missing parts of my feminine self. I had lived from the neck up—a true daughter of Zeus, like Athene, born from his head. Well-educated and working in intellectual arenas, I realized I was estranged from my feeling self and my body—the realm of the feminine.

In the third dream of this early triptych, a beautiful, young Polynesian woman smiled broadly at me. In that smile, I felt her acceptance and encouragement, calling me further into that vibrancy of life I was longing for. She was very much at home in her body and imbued with feeling and self-assuredness. I would learn that she was my projection for a greater sense of wholeness and self-worth. I thought this was perhaps a premonitory dream assuring me that revivification may be the result of this inner journey.

Stranger in a Strange Land

Several years later, the dream image of this Polynesian woman inspired me to make a stop to Bali as part of a larger trip already planned. I rented an open jeep and proceeded to explore this beautiful Indonesian island, taking in the sights and sounds of daily life there. The paved road from the largest city, Denpasar, eventually became a dirt road that led me deeper into the center of the island, which became less populated and more rural. I drove through several small villages and noticed that at the heart of each was an open-aired temple, usually of Hindu origin, with numerous wall carvings of figures sacred to this religion. I drove by people on the road, many of whom were women carrying tall, colorful stacks of food and fresh flowers on their heads, some as tall or taller than the women who bore them. These were religious offerings the women took to the temples at the end of the day in thanksgiving to the gods for their daily bounties. They reminded me of my dream image of the Polynesian woman.

I smiled and waved as I passed by, and they smiled and waved back. I saw a woman sitting on the porch of a small wooden hut, smoking a wooden pipe. I wondered what she was smoking and noted that this was not typical in the U.S. This was indeed a very different culture from mine—and I was fascinated by it and the people. One of the most startling differences was that the women here, in contrast to those in the city, were wearing no blouses or tops: They wore sarongs, long skirts that went from their waists nearly to their ankles, but they were bare-breasted. Some were barefoot; some wore flat, well-worn sandals.

I continued to drive further and noticed I was coming into a deep forest area. It was beginning to rain and get dark. Suddenly, the road came to an end. I was disappointed that I could not go further but also a bit relieved, for I was becoming more aware of my situation. I was a young, attractive, blonde-haired American woman out in the middle of the deepest part of a foreign and very nature-bound land, where the English language was not predominant. I began to feel somewhat unsafe in this paradisiacal bliss. Despite the warm smiles and welcoming gestures of the Balinese people, I knew I was not one of them. In fact, I was the stranger here. We came from very different worlds. Yet, I felt a deep affinity for them as fellow human beings.

It began to rain harder, and, as I drove back out of the forest, I passed on the road an older woman who wore only a sarong around her waist. She was barefoot and bare-breasted. She wore her greying long, black hair in an untidy bun and carried a single basket on top of her head. What was so striking about this Balinese woman was that she had only one disproportionately elongated breast. She had no right breast, only something that looked like a reconstructed nipple on her chest, and her left breast drooped well below her waist. It was a startling sight, and I turned quickly as I passed to make sure that I had, in fact, seen her. Tears streamed down my face as I drove away. I longed to talk to her: I imagined that she could tell me secret things. She seemed to carry herself with such dignity! She did not feel a need to cover her body, and I wondered if she belonged to a special cult of women which required this type of badge of honor. I also wondered if she had been a victim of breast cancer. This woman stirred something deep within me. I felt a strong desire to connect with her. These projections I was unconsciously making upon this woman served to help awaken in me a powerful force of connection with my own sense of the feminine within.

Later, I recalled the death from breast cancer of my paternal grandmother. This was the time prior to modern chemotherapy and examination techniques, and she'd had to undergo a radical mastectomy. One day she showed me her body. The entire right side of her chest had been removed, so much so that I could see several of her ribs and the area where some had been removed along with her right breast. I was a young girl of sixteen, and this was a very shocking sight to see! I loved my grandmother deeply, and I felt her cavernous shame and sadness at the loss of who she felt herself to be.

The contrast between the Balinese woman, who seemed confident and dignified, and my grandmother, who conveyed deep shame and sadness, has stayed with me and remains vivid. I thought that perhaps the Balinese woman may have felt contained enough in her environment and her culture, as well as in the surrounding natural world, to simply be as she was, who she was, regardless of her physical disfiguration; whereas, my grandmother felt estranged from her body, her sense of self and her outer community.

I wondered about the difference it might have made for my grandmother had she been regarded by her family, friends, and community as a great woman granted wisdom by God through her affliction. I had told my grandmother it did not matter what she looked like, because I loved her. Although these words had soothed her, I could see that she'd felt deeply wounded in her most feminine being. I felt helpless to give her back what she felt she had lost. The stature of the more self-assured Balinese woman has remained a strong imprint. She continues to emerge, particularly when I am feeling a loss of self-confidence and need assurance and encouragement to move forward with the task at hand.

As I continued working with my dreams and deepening my commitment to my inner life, I discovered that part of what I was missing was more of a one-on-one quality of relating to and working with others, rather than the more collective group or team work in which I was engaged in my outer life. This led me to seek further training to become a psychotherapist. I returned to school for a master's degree in social work and spent another two years in a Washington, D.C., clinical setting, seeing individuals who were dually-diagnosed with mental illness and substance abuse issues. After obtaining a license to practice, I opened my own private practice. But still, I felt there was more to do.

Something I couldn't name seemed to be moving me along, and each time I questioned the direction I was taking, a dream would emerge and a feeling would urge me onward. I decided to seek further training to become a Jungian analyst and went to Zürich to study at the C. G. Jung Institute-Zürich. I found myself at once thrilled to be there among others from many different nations but also confronted with tremendous doubt every day. Everything was strange—the language of Swiss German, the exactitude of time, place, and behavioral expectations, the high cost of living, and many other issues of living there. Despite this daily doubt, there was also an underlying feeling of surety that this was right for me. I was again sorting seeds. I kept going.

Strangers in a Strange Land

After completing my coursework at the Jung Institute, I had a couple of months to wait before the graduation ceremony. I heard about a small group of students taking a trip to Egypt led by one of the analysts from the German program at the Institute. I leapt at the chance to join them. I was the only English-speaking member of the group, and I wondered if it would be a good-enough fit. I asked the leader what she thought. She said the guides in Egypt all knew English, so it wouldn't be a problem. And so, I went. We were one of the first tour groups to return on what was the one-year anniversary date following the 1998 assassinations of a predominantly Swiss group by extreme Muslim terrorists. Our group's intent was, in part, to show a refusal to be intimidated by the terrorists. This was five years after the first World Trade Center bombing in 1993 and two years before the 9/11 airplane bombings of the World Trade Center twin towers in 2001—a time of great political tension and unrest.

Despite the unrest and potential danger, I wanted to see Egypt and to explore the ancient world of the pharaohs and the mysterious hieroglyphs. I was very intrigued about the symbols, particularly on the theme of life after death, that arrayed the tombs in the Valley of the Kings, and what they meant on the more psychological and religious levels. I thought this would be my best, if not only, opportunity to travel there, especially with a group of like-minded psychologists. We arrived at night with a rather bumpy landing in Luxor and were all crammed into two cars for our destination. The bumpy landing metaphorically described how things would proceed throughout my trip.

I understood nothing that was being said between our leader and the driver as they spoke in German and Arabic. And one woman who did speak English was not very good at relaying to me a real-time, blow-by-blow of the conversation. To add to my discomfort and confusion, we were not traveling along paved, lighted highways but on dirt roads with the car lights off. It felt unsafe, especially since I could see the main highway running parallel to the dirt road. The explanation given was that it was done to save battery life, which might very well have been true. However, I also surmised that we were not supposed to be "off-the-grid" as security was tight and all tourists were directed to a handful of hotels, where they could be monitored for their safety and for the safety of the Egyptian people. Actually, I was not fully aware that we would be staying with a family in their home. I assumed we would be staying in hotels.

We arrived around midnight at the house of the Egyptian family with whom we were staying in a small, Muslim village near the Valley of the Kings. We were greeted by Zaineb, the mother of the household, and other family members. All the women were dressed in the traditional Muslim black dress, the abaya, and the young man wore a galabiya, a long-sleeved, loose-fitting robe that hung from neck to foot. My room was the nearest to the only minaret on the West Bank, from which prayers were being called out continuously for the first three days we were there. A prominent member of the village had just died, and these continuous prayers were part of the religious ritual. Though similar in some respects to my experiences in Bali, the sights, sounds, tastes, and smells were very foreign to me, and I felt truly out of my element.

By day, we began our touring. Although I was happy to be with the group, who were very polite and pleasant, they seemed to forget that I knew no Swiss German and really didn't respond when I brought it to their attention. Our leader, who was supposed to provide English translations, made little if any attempt to do so and would only give me cursory, terse summaries. It was clear that I was to just go along with the program and not make a fuss. I knew I needed to find my own way.

In the evenings our hosts, the mother Zaineb, her fifteen-year-old daughter, and Zaineb's mother-in-law, cooked delicious homemade meals, and we dined al fresco around a long wooden table enjoying the cool evening breezes and star-covered sky. That first evening, the group talked about the day's experiences, but, again, as much as I tried to join in, my interactions were very limited due to the language barrier. I had never felt so out of place—a stranger, myself, not only in this very different Egyptian culture, but also in the group I was with, which also included people from a different culture with a different language.

On the second evening, I discovered that the seventeen-year-old son, Mohammed, spoke English. After the women served the group and then retreated to the kitchen or other areas of the house, we ate dinner, and afterwards, our group began to discuss the events of the day. Since they were speaking Swiss German with no translation, I broke ranks and joined Mohammed, who sat quietly on a nearby bench. I started by asking him to translate what they were saying, but then we began to have our own conversation about his life, his family, and about Egyptian life in general. Although this dialogue was frowned upon by our leader, I think she realized it was better than having to make further accommodations for my needs; consequently, talking with Mohammed became my evening ritual. Eros was alive and well, helping me to navigate the choppy waters of language and group expectations.

During our daily tours, I found English-speaking guides at the places we visited. At the end of the week, most of the group returned to Zürich, but I signed up to stay a second week, as I knew I would not return to Egypt any time soon, if ever. It turned out that no one else was staying except the leader.

After the group left, the leader and I ate dinner together, during which time she spoke English and I relayed to her my impressions of the tour. She expressed sorrow that I was not able to share more with the group because of the language issue and then said she had some things to tell me about my stay for the next week. She proceeded to give me some "Dos and Don'ts" about how I was to travel around. It was clear she was not interested in doing anything together and that, essentially, I was on my own. She warned that women were not allowed to go out of the home after dark, nor were they to have contact with men. She added other admonitions I understood as rules of protection, and I thanked her for her concern.

Then, she left to travel, and I remained with Zaineb's family. I really wasn't sure what I was going to do on my own, but I did know I wanted to return to the tomb of Queen Nefertiti and to see more of the Valley of the Kings. In the late 90s there were no smartphones, so I just set out on my own, hoping for the best. I managed pretty well but always felt uncomfortable without a constant guide or someone to accompany me.

The night after the group left and we were finishing dinner, Mohammed asked if I would go on a walk with him. Remembering the words of the leader, I told him that I didn't think it was a good idea. He asked in a commanding voice, "Why not?!" His mother was nearby, so I asked her to join us for my explanation to Mohammed and asked him to translate to her. She sat silently as I told them what the leader had told me. I noticed she was frowning and grimacing as I relayed to them the leader's rules.

Suddenly, Zaineb stood up, banged her fist on the table, and exclaimed, "Rubbish!" This reaction startled me because I had never seen her so animated nor heard her utter any word beyond the Arabic language. I wondered what had been so upsetting to cause this outburst when she, at once, asked me to go for a walk with her!

I accepted immediately. She donned her veil, or hijab, and we began our walk. It was a beautiful, warm evening with a gentle breeze blowing. As we walked, I felt the awkwardness and frustration of not being able to talk with her, but this did not seem important to her. I made a motion with my arms about the dry, warm breeze. She smiled in acknowledgement, took in a deep breath and said, "Hoa." That was Arabic for "wind" as well as "breath." I thought of the wind as the breath of God and responded with the Hebrew word "ruach." She nodded and I smiled.

Although I thought we were just out for an evening stroll, she had something else in mind. We started out along the main paved road in the area, but few cars and little activity were apparent during that evening hour, so I felt a bit apprehensive. Suddenly, she grabbed my sleeve and pulled me onto a dirt road. Now it was even darker with no street lights. Despite my warm feeling for her, I began to feel more anxious and very out of place. I heard a donkey braying, some chickens clucking, and a few other animal noises on my left as we walked, but it was too dark to see even any outlines of these animals. Then I saw to my right a vague shape of a crudely built clay wall. Zaineb started speaking Arabic to someone, and I heard one or more men's voices on the other side of the wall. I could feel my fear increasing and irrationally wondered if I was to become the next hostage/victim of a planned plot. Strangeness lends itself to projections of our worst fears, and I was in full-on projection mode!

Shortly, we arrived at a group of clay buildings. Zaineb knocked on the door of one of them, and a young woman answered. A little boy came running to her side and his eyes grew very large; he screamed and began to cry. That scream brought three other women to the door. It seems that I was the first white woman the boy had seen in their home. I soon realized this was Zaineb's childhood home: These women were her mother and sisters.

After the women calmed the boy and put him to bed, they joined me in their living room and graciously brought me a cup of karkade, the Egyptian tea offered to all guests. As I took in my surroundings, I noticed a framed photo of an older man, smiling broadly, that was hung prominently above the mantle. I suspected that he was the patriarch of the family, which was confirmed later by Mohammed. He had passed some years before. This picture made me feel welcomed, and I began to feel more at ease and at home there.

Since I did not understand a word of Arabic, I sat and sipped my tea as the sisters spoke about what I guessed was a problem of the day, and their mother sat, listening intently. Clearly, they wanted their mother's advice on how to deal with the problem. I noticed that the sisters talked and then stopped, waited, and listened to their mother's reactions. It was clear they held deep respect for her.

After a while, they turned and smiled at me. My friend got up, and I knew it was time to leave. They each gave me a hug and let me know I was accepted and welcome in their home at any time. I asked Mohammed about this event the next day, and he said that his mother had felt offended by the leader's comments, which she felt prevented tourists from really getting to know the local villagers. I was moved by this and felt certain that other women in my cultural milieu would have had a similar reaction. We weren't that different after all.

The following day, as I was returning home from a long, hot day of touring, a pickup truck passed with about six women in the back of it. They were all dressed in the black covering from head to toe. I recognized Zaineb and, as the truck stopped, she invited me to join them. I gratefully accepted but felt out of place in my t-shirt and jeans, so I motioned with a smile and joking gesture that I needed a head covering like theirs. Immediately, one of the women pulled out an extra head covering and gave it to me to wear! We all burst out laughing as I proceeded to put it on. What a sight I must have been! I no longer felt like a stranger with the women of this village. After two weeks of confusing interactions,

I felt a deep appreciation for their gift of laughter, inclusion, and, ultimately, acceptance.

These experiences in Egypt, initially among strangers from a very different culture, with differing customs, dress, and language, carried a deep undercurrent of Eros. They may have been strangers to me, but I, too, was a stranger to them, and, in fact, I was discovering more strangeness within myself. I asked myself: Who was I, really? I identified as Christian in my beliefs and American in upbringing, but these women were just as devoted to their beliefs and customs, and it felt like, despite these differences, we shared the same human values of courtesy, respect, integrity, acceptance, and love. As I grappled with the frustrations and inability to express myself through language, I felt the presence of Eros in the strong desire, the need, to relate to both these Egyptian and Swiss strangers. Eros was inviting me deeper to confront shadow material within, such as my unexamined racial, political, and religious biases. This strong urge led me along this path of strangeness, and I followed—consciously aware of the danger that persisted. And, through the strangeness, I was discovering how alive I felt.

On my final day I decided to go further south to see the Aswan Dam and to experience the Nubian culture. I was not aware that this area might be exposing me to greater danger due to civil disturbances just across the border in Sudan. I hired a driver, and we joined a caravan of cars for security reasons, which were unknown to me at the time. There was one caravan in the morning and one returning around 5:30 p.m. My driver, who disappeared for a brief time, returned, but was too late to join the caravan. This meant we would have to stay overnight. I felt uneasy and thought it was too much of a risk, so I managed to get a ticket on the last train back to Luxor. I was the only woman in the car of foreign men and felt the threat of danger at this time. After a short while, a man came and sat next to me; he talked with me in his broken English. Despite my apprehension about his intentions, I also felt relieved and protected by his presence. We arrived in Luxor shortly before midnight. Before we parted ways, he invited me to a wedding in his village, and I profusely thanked him for the invitation and for accompanying me on the journey.

I realized as I stood in the middle of the train station that I did not have an address for Zaineb's house. Our leader had never given it to us, and I stood there, wondering what to do. The taxis I had hired in the area had always picked me up at the house, stayed with me throughout the day, and known where to drop me back home. As I looked for a taxi, suddenly, out of the shadows, a strange man approached me. No, it was not a stranger. It was Mohammed! I was astonished to see him since there could have been no way he would have known where I was or when I was returning. When I asked him, he simply smiled impishly. To this day, I have no idea how he found me.

Egypt was an extremely powerful example of how Eros can serve as a bridge to the stranger that in turn can lead to further self-development and life renewal. The irony is that I went to learn more about my fascination with the ancient Egyptian world, yet it was my experiences with the present-day Egyptian people that made the more lasting impressions on me. These experiences affected the way that I see and relate to others and how I learned to integrate very divergent, strange ways and unconscious contents that, once explored, led to greater empathy, self-confidence, and a deeper affinity with others. The negative, even arrogant, judgments I made out of fear or preconceived ideas were unfinished tasks calling me to the stranger—and Eros took me there.

These experiences of Eros and the stranger have also helped me to be a better analyst—to see my clients, all initially strangers—in more empathic and receptive ways. I have learned to recognize projections quicker, allowing me to really see past stereotypes and to connect with the stranger through Eros. As I am completing these musings, I realize that Eros has been with me all along, even in the darkness, as my companion and guide.

*****

Two months after this trip, on my graduation day in Zürich, I was preparing to leave my room for the ceremony when, suddenly, I felt strange, like something was falling off me. If I were a snake, the sensation would have announced the shedding of a skin. I felt completely exposed and went back into my room and closed the door. I wondered what was happening, but I knew what it was: My old identity and sense of self were falling away. This was the *real* graduation. I opened the door and walked out into my strange and newly transformed life.

Eros Returns

The ancient Greek poet Sappho remarks, "Eros seizes and shakes my very soul like the wind on the mountains shaking ancient oaks" (Philoctetes, 2008).

Reflecting on past experiences has a way of helping us to appreciate and perhaps re-value our life moments as well as propelling us into future endeavors. But what is it that moves us to do so? Chance encounters with strangers can nourish and enrich our lives immensely. And it is Eros, the Greek god of desirous relatedness, who symbolically represents that inner, intense drive that connects us with those we do not know as well as with the unknown, the strangers within.

I regard Eros as the initiator of connectedness, with intensity and often urgency, like a bridge to our greater Self and to others. I felt this connection with the strange-looking woman on the road in Bali and in my deep desire to speak with her. I thought there was much to learn from her—her secrets, her wisdom about all things feminine. Her uninhibited openness with her body, in contrast to the shame my grandmother felt from breast removal, was helping me realize my own way of seeing my body and how I regarded it. In my culture and milieu, a woman's body was viewed more as an object of desire to be possessed rather than a part of a whole, separate individual to be seen in her own right. My work included bringing head and body together, which led me to a greater ability to express my thoughts and feelings in a more embodied way. In short, I was feeling greater freedom to be my authentic self and to feel comfortable in my own skin! Eros led me to the strangeness that became self-knowledge and the ability to embrace my own inner beauty, leading to a greater sense of fulfillment and joy. When we reach this place within ourselves, there is a real sense of freedom to be one's self, and others will see it, too.

In contrast with logos, which Jung identified as the principle of knowledge and discernment, he described Eros as psychic energy, in general, and the principle of relatedness, in particular. In *Memories, Dreams, Reflections*, Jung remarked:

> *Love "bears all things" and "endures all things" (1 Cor. 13:7). These words say all there is to be said; nothing can be added to them. For we are in the deepest sense the victims and the instruments of cosmogonic "love." I put the word in quotation marks to indicate that I do not use it in its connotations of desiring, preferring, favoring, wishing, and similar feelings, but as something superior to the individual, a unified and undivided whole. Being a part, man cannot grasp the whole. He is at its mercy. He may assent to it, or rebel against it; but he is always caught up by it and enclosed within it. He is dependent upon it and is sustained by it. Love is his light and his darkness, whose end he cannot see. "Love ceases not".... If he possesses a grain of wisdom, he will lay down his arms*

> *and name the unknown by the more unknown, ignotum per ignotius—that is, by the name of God. (Jung, 1961/1989, p. 354)*

More succinctly put, Jung believed the principle of Eros to be the *desire* for wholeness, even wholeness itself, extending beyond that of the individual. It may initially take the form of passionate love, but it is more truly a desire for "psychic relatedness," a desire for interconnection within parts of ourselves, as well as more empathic, qualitative interactions with others.

When beginning this chapter, it was my intent to provide short vignettes of Eros-like experiences with those initially unknown to me—strangers. It was to be like the Roman form of Eros, the Hallmark version of the winged, cute Cupid with his little quiver of love arrows, shooting them with his bow, adept in his aim and intent to spread his sparks of love wherever he chose. Indeed, our war-weary world could use many arrows of love and joy right now, and this is part of Cupid's job—to unite us. But I discovered, as I struggled to capture the essence of Eros, that Cupid and the greeting-card version of sweetness and light were not really doing justice to this mighty god and the incredible energy he embodies.

This particular description of Eros was aptly captured by Australian journalist and writer Brigid Delaney after she was seized by the energy of this mighty god in an experience she had upon emerging from the pandemic:

> *It was June 2020, really early in the morning, still dark around the edges, and I was crossing the big intersection at Spencer and Bourke streets in Melbourne.*
>
> *I was half asleep and the only people around were tradies [i.e., tradesmen]. At the other end of the*

> *crossing, I locked eyes with one of them and, out of nowhere, suddenly felt weak with lust.*
> *The whole thing - the whole long, loaded glance - only lasted a few seconds, until the lights changed and the road was crossed. But more than a year later I still remember the intensity of the feeling.*
> *It was a blast of pure eros. Every cell was lit up. If it had been possible to just do it in the middle of the road with this yellow-vest stranger, I would have.*
> *At Spencer Street, I caught my train, settled in and then proceeded to ask myself over the course of the 11-hour journey: what the hell was that? What just happened? My body was communicating something - but why was the feeling so overwhelming? (Delaney, 2021)*

We see from Delaney's engaging description of her powerful encounter with Eros how inner material can seek an outer other or stranger to grab our attention, to reveal itself for further understanding of ourselves. Perhaps Delaney felt much like Psyche in the dark, with an instantaneously instinctual strong sexual attraction that can lead us to even deeper awareness of the stranger within and without. Jung was well aware of the power of Eros when he quoted the Renaissance scholar, Erasmus, who in turn borrowed from the Delphic oracle the wise words: "Called or uncalled, God is present!" (Jung, 1978, p. 164). He had this quote placed over the threshold of his door in Küsnacht and on his tombstone.

In Jungian psychology, the unconscious is this strange land—a world of Eros and of dreams that carry powerful archetypal images that can shape our lives and move us forward. The stranger as symbol, as in the pivotal dreams I shared, can serve as that which is emotionally rich and super-charged with the energy needed to transform us into greater wholeness. Little had I realized at that time that my dreams would lead to connecting me with other aspects of myself through the strangers in my inner and outer worlds.

As I was completing these musings on Eros and the stranger, and after an unexpectedly deep, inward encounter with both, Eros returned. In fact, I wonder whether he was really gone. Even in my darkness, in my felt estrangement which this writing task revealed, I'd turned to the myth of Eros and Psyche, relying on Psyche's completion of Aphrodite's tasks and the lysis in the myth of reunion with Eros. Initially, Psyche felt Eros to be a mysterious sexual partner and was somewhat content. But through the visits with her sisters, those nattering voices of doubt and curiosity, she was prompted to take a deeper look. As with Psyche, I found myself in a strange, unknown place and needed to learn to discern what was important and what was not; to become more conscious of the deeper aspects of myself. Only then could I begin to feel the presence of Eros, who was always there.

Often, if not always, Eros comes first as a stranger or the strange, the new, the different, the odd. And if we can tolerate this mighty force, if we can embrace him, we become transformed by the experience into greater aspects of our being—strange states of life, beauty, love, even joy.

Eros knows the darkest depths and the brightest heavenly heights of the soul, of Psyche. Words of poetry or other art forms such as music best capture this mighty god's superordinate force within us. And dreams invite that force into our sleep. Old feminine attitudes with broken legs, mountain women carved by the Self, Kore qualities of the Polynesian smile—all beckon relationship. But, also, we glimpse Eros in the song without words, like the laughter with the women in the truck; the overpowering rush of pure feeling, like Zaineb's cry of "Rubbish"; or the stranger that was Mohammed appearing out of the shadows when I was lost and wondering how to return home. Like an undertow, this force pulls us out of our ego-selves down into deeper waters, onto the roads to foreign places like Bali or into the darkness of Egyptian nights.

Strange Indeed

The first time I felt lost and void of feeling and connection, in my early thirties, I did not know what I was missing or how to find it. I was ill-equipped to deal with the deadness or what to do about it. This led me to Jungian analysis and the work with strange dream images and mythological symbols that helped me find Eros and discover the feminine aspects of myself. It was the world of the feminine that I met as the stranger: Hers is the world of emotions and feelings, of valuation, of the instincts and the body. This world involves connectedness and a relatedness to and empathy for ourselves and others. I had become a true obedient daughter of the world of logos, of patriarchal ideas, principles, and laws that had obscured and truncated my feminine self. Contrary to the masculine principle of doing, which I already did quite well, the feminine principle concerns being and becoming. That was foreign to me.

The myth of Psyche and Eros helped me develop and recover various aspects of my personality unknown to me. Psyche sorted seeds while she waited in agonizing anticipation for the reunion with Eros. And in waiting, as in pregnancy, something is forming, developing in order to be born.

What I knew during this recent time of melancholy and emptiness, which I had learned through my first experience of it, was that I had to wait and sort the seeds. Then just as suddenly as Eros had left, he re-emerged, effecting a greater sense of depth and fullness through my reflections and writing.

As I was completing the final edits for this story, a strange event occurred. I had left the cold and snowy winter of my home in Arlington, Virginia, for a six-month's stay in the warmer climes of the Florida panhandle; ironically, a very unexpected snowstorm and wintery blast of low temperatures whipped through this area on January 22nd. I was utterly shocked and surprised with such a unique occurrence, even in January, in the sunshine state. But strangely, I felt alive again!

It was as if Eros had affirmed the deep inner work I had been concentrating on with an outer exclamation of renewal and beauty that a heavy, white blanket of snow can bring. When Psyche was reunited with Eros, they ascended together to the heights of Mt. Olympus, and Psyche gave birth to their female child and named her Pleasure. Through my relationship with Eros and the stranger, I have discovered great pleasure and joy—and a revivification of life!

Training in Love

Marilyn Marshall

Sometimes love looks and feels like we imagine it does. Sometimes, it does not. Sometimes it is more. Invites more. Demands more—of us.

I met her in June of 2008 ... in a dream.
She was a killer with a knife
She was crazy—this short, squat old woman—
Whinnying like a horse.
She didn't speak—she just whinnied in this high-pitched manic sort of a way.
So, I did what anyone would do—
I called the police
And they came—
Handcuffed her and took her away.
It was a dream.
But then I wondered about her—
What it would be like to be her ...
To be a crazed woman who thought she was a horse.
So, in my imagination, I climbed on a chestnut mare
And rode bareback through a grassy field.
The horse galloped with long powerful strides
As if she had just been set loose from ages of confinement.
So, I crouched close to her
My head right above her thick, sweating, solid neck

And as the wind whipped her mane and my hair
Her mane *became* my hair
And it was as if I were the horse.
I felt these sensations in my chest
Expanding with muscle and bone and pumping heart
And tears filled my eyes
Flowing with the sadness
That I had never felt this free
And the joy
That I felt it now.
I wanted to rear up, to stand majestically on hind legs in a posture of power and purpose, and make that sound the crazy woman made.
Then, suddenly, I was standing in a large opening of what seemed to be
A cave
A fire was burning, and an old woman was sitting beside it.
The horse, already there, was standing in the shadows.
I could see her chestnut coat glistening in the flickers of light.
"Sit down," the woman demanded. "This is not an invitation."
"I have been waiting here your whole life."
She looked angrily from me to the snake she was roasting over the fire—sliced lengthwise and skewered on a pointed stick that somehow did not burn.
I followed the nod of her head and sat across from her.
Strangely, I wanted to know her.
She took a bite of the snake and offered the stick to me.
I, too, took a bite of the charred, rubbery reptile.
Smoke rose from this fire and dissipated somewhere above, and she began drawing in the dirt—a cross of two equal lines and then four concentric circles on top

of it. She did this slowly, placing the smallest, central circle at the point where the horizontal and vertical lines met and moved out from there.

She stared at me, the kind of stare I wanted to turn from but knew I needed to meet: "You think this life belongs to all these others. It does not. It belongs only to you. I have not remained so that you could give yourself away."

She pointed to the center circle. "I am here." Then she placed her finger on the outlying circle where the number two would be on the face of a clock. "And you are here."

Her eyes were resolute. "Man is only man. You have relegated your life to such restriction. Don't you know that I had to come—had to give you more? I sit alone in this cave, and I think of you. I light the fire; I draw your images. I eat snake, and I wait for you to finally come. Your love has been so confined, so strangled, and you have kept yourself hidden—from me. I have not been hiding. I am you, and I am in this state out of your neglect."

"I am so sorry," I whispered.

"Never mind that now. Now it begins."

We left the cave and began to walk together in silence. She was on my left and carried a tall walking stick. She knew the earth, the trees and rocks. She was at home here—with the flowers and the thorns, the rivers and seas—and the mountains and valleys—as if she was the lone woman. Looking out over the expanse or enclosed in the evergreen thickness, she was one with it all. At the beginning and at the end—all life was here, and my heart expanded in gratitude just to Be—with her.

I will never forget that dream. I will never forget her, the crazy woman who was a killer with a knife and whinnied like a horse. I'd avoided her at first; she repulsed me. I had been in analysis with a male analyst for twelve years, and, after his death in 2006, I entered analysis with a female analyst. By 2008, I had been a candidate-in-training for six years and was in what was termed the "control stage" of training, finalizing my thesis and cases for exams the following spring. I would graduate in April 2009. This said, of course I knew better than to avoid or rationalize her. My unadulterated emotional response, itself, was a clear indication that this feminine figure was an unknown aspect of myself and held, along with that knife, a great deal of psychic energy.

My usual response to dreams, after working with associations and exploring amplifications, was to honor the dream by writing

Whinnying Woman

prose or poetry, by sculpting with clay or using pastels or paint to create an image or feeling from the dream. For this bizarre female figure, I quickly scribbled with brown pastels an ugly, horse-faced human head with horse ears (the "Whinnying Woman" image) and shuttered her away in my dream art folder. Days later, after active imagination, I carefully painted with water colors our time together—the cave, the wise, old Whinnying Woman in ancient, earthy garb, sans horse face, the fire and roasted snake, her cross and circles in the dirt, her place in the center circle and mine on the outer one, and, finally, unconsciously and automatically, I'd painted a large, diamond-shaped marker on the ground outside the cave (the "Whinnying Woman 2" image). I had no idea, then, why

Whinnying Woman 2

I placed that diamond in this scene—only that it belonged there, too.

Circles of time later, I would remember why: When I was a little girl, I would use full sheets of looseleaf paper to draw large, basic diamond shapes, dividing the inner space into very small pieces, much like stained-glass window panes, and then shading them with a multitude of bright Crayola crayons. I was, unconsciously, creating mandalas, geometric figures that had had a centering, containing focus during a crowded, chaotic, and insecure childhood. Remembering what she'd said about being with me my entire life and then painting my images, how could I not have added the stained-glass diamond, this one, not the multitude of myriad colors but the central radiation of four orange and four royal blue triangles? And because I don't understand how to depict depth perception, I had to paint her mandala image in the sky with a glowing, fiery background instead of on the cave's hallowed ground; nevertheless, we both knew where and to whom it belonged. Archetypal Self-symbols, she and the mandala of that watercolor painting still sit framed and solitary on my bedside table.

Transformed through our relatedness from the crazed Whinnying Woman, this wise old woman's final words, "Now it begins," both were and were not surprising: Now it begins? I had had quite a few new beginnings in my adult life by 2008. But when I considered the timing of the dream and active imagination, I had associated my final year's tasks in training. I was not at the beginning—I was, hopefully, at the end. However, because of the numinosity of the experience, and because I understood this archetypal feminine figure as a Self-image, I believed her remark had a deeper meaning. I would begin again, begin this next task of circumambulation with a more conscious relationship to this deep feminine presence and her remarks about love. In part, I would learn to precisely wield one of her instruments, the knife, not without incurring cuts and wounds in the process—and I would eat snake.

> *You think this life belongs to all these others. It does not. It belongs only to you.*

Born in 1951, I grew up during a time when the millennia-old patriarchal structures, laws, and attitudes were prioritized, promoted, and upheld, while the collective rested on these laurels in pacified agreement with *Father Knows Best*, a popular television series of that decade (Rodney, 1954–1960), among similar others, characterizing the supreme value of the male and his weighted majority in programming, leading, and presiding. Men and the masculine principles prevailing were the authority, the "heads" of the divinely endowed religions and churches; of the federal, state, and local governing bodies; of family, of academia, of professions, work forces, organizations, etc. I'd taken my place under the "truth" of that one-sided, hierarchical belief system despite my early experiences to the contrary: My father proved consistently that he did not know best, and both my paternal grandfather's silently strict demands and my maternal grandfather's periodically volatile rages enlisted order through fear. Egg-shell walking became a cultivated talent. Nevertheless, I, too, learned and adopted an overvaluation of man, male and "father" knowing best: first, as a pleasing child to a father overtaken by alcohol and a mother devoured by motherhood; as the oldest grandchild, the eldest of eleven children, and as a second mother to my siblings. Then, as a wife, college graduate, mother of three sons, creator of youth programs for the Catholic Church, and religion teacher for a Catholic girls' high school, I continued the obedience and conformity to a particular image of this ruling, masculine principle ... until my forty-ish year.

> *I have not remained so that you could give yourself away. Man is only man.*

An unconscious rebellion, hints of which had been appearing and gathering strength for a few years, rose up within me and breached patriarchal boundaries, confronted expected acquiescence, weakened unquestioned beliefs, and demanded attention at home and in work. Old conscious patterns of perfectionistic doing and stunted relating through the aegis of a dogmatic masculine, and a particular feminine attitude accompanying it, began a decline as I felt the intimations of something other than what I knew myself to be. The psychic energy of the Kore emerging in me and alive in the adolescent girls I was teaching infused new life; the new relationships with other women teaching in the school, their different ages, stories, personalities, and perspectives, opened windows; the contemplative experiences at my yearly silent retreats, one in particular with a nun who led a guided meditation for us to meet "the feminine face" of God, encouraged my exploration and creation, along with a colleague, of a feminine spirituality course for high school seniors. Although still a formidable personal influence, the supreme authority of men and fathers began to weaken. I had begun to listen differently, open less guardedly; play and create and connect with an other something within—all the while walking a razor's edge with the Church's acceptable "feminine face" of God our father on one side, and the ancient cultural traditions of the divine feminine, the Goddess, on the other—quite a tension for a few years. And surprisingly supportive of these and other rebellious hints was an unconventional yet traditionally instructed masculine—one of those "fathers" of the church—an elderly Jesuit priest at the women's retreat center who'd agreed to be my spiritual director. He introduced me to the *Spiritual Exercises of Ignatius Loyola* and the tarot—quite a duo, yes?

I was thirty-seven at the time, and when I first visited this playful priest in colorful suspenders, he'd asked if I'd had a dream. I'd had one the previous night that had a deep impact on me and introduced me to what I would learn, years later, was the numinous experience of an archetype:

> *I was standing outside my house looking up into the sunny sky, and suddenly there appeared, within what seemed like a column in mid-air, pastel-colored clouds on which words were printed, moving upwards as if on a printing press. I was amazed! The movement of words was so swift, I could only make out two: "God" and "unity." Then, suddenly, I was flipped upside down by an invisible force and was suspended in mid-air with my legs in a stork pose, my long hair draping my head and my arms dangling down towards the ground. My brother, who I guess had been standing nearby, reached up and pulled me right-side up and feet on the ground, and my grandfather, who had died years earlier, came out of the house and angrily yelled, "Goddammit, get in here!"*

After listening to the dream, he nodded and walked to his window, pulled a round card from the fanned-out deck on the table, and handed it to me. "Is this what you looked like in the dream?" The "Hanged One," one of the major arcana of the tarot. (In most traditional tarot decks, I'd later learn, that card is called The Hanged Man, but this was the Motherpeace deck (Vogel & Noble, 1981). It depicted a woman hanging mid-air, upside down with a blue snake wrapped around her ankle connecting her to the branch of a tree.) I was unaware of the tarot, and, although there was no snake or tree in my dream image, I felt a sudden chill seeing the image and responded with a nod to his question. He quietly remarked that my world was being turned upside down. Indeed!

As I said, the duo: During this time, I'd had a deeply meaningful experience with one of the meditations in the *Spiritual Exercises* that focused on Jesus in Gethsemane. In my meditation I was moved to tears for the depth of Christ's anguish. In spite of his terrible fear, his felt aloneness, and his agonizing entreaty to God, he shouldered his truth, not another's: He followed his individual path, not his religion's, his culture's—not a path expected and imagined by those who loved him. I feared and desired the same—living my truth, one that was revealing values and principles other than those I had adopted.

You have relegated your life to such restriction.

I'd fallen in love my first year in college; he was in his third. Eros had released a powerful arrow: a different feeling than high school crushes, sexual awakening, and dating. Initially, the chemistry was there, but, as we got to know each other, I was drawn also to his unquestionable faith in God. Married two years later, after he graduated, we settled in the city where he'd been raised, the oldest son of five children of devout Catholic parents, and where I finished college. He'd constellated a spiritual desire I had denounced as a child, and so I followed his path and adopted his allegiance to the Catholic Church—for about twenty years.

My enthusiastic involvement in the Church felt meaningful, especially because creative ideas, a dynamic quality of my intuition, flowed abundantly and met the needs of young people in the parish and archdiocese. In retrospect, I realize the order and stability essential to my husband and fundamental in the Church had provided a compensation for the "missing" father and the chaos of my childhood and adolescence. Yet both of them "knowing what was best" and rejecting what interfered maintained a familiar pattern I continued to follow. Later, after much work in analysis, I would naturally have to face my shadow aspects, complexes, and defenses in relation to my compliance. But I think the most difficult confrontation I faced was in the gradual consciousness of my projections of the dogmatic and critical masculine. Not that there wasn't a hook for and reality in those projections, but the truly destructive and insidious pronouncements were those that sounded against me: thoughts in my "head," a negative animus held court for the prosecution of whatever it deemed a threat to its position of control. Relating to this power within was a daunting challenge awaiting me, but I didn't know that then.

By the time of the *Exercises*, the stirring had been happening, and I had begun to silently question, doubt, and disagree, not only with my husband and the Church, but with the culture's patriarchal beliefs and attitudes—more specifically, those that fostered the devaluation of the feminine. Consequently, I wanted to discern my own faith and question and consider my own experiences, thoughts, and feelings. I wanted to claim my truth—at least the seeds of that truth. This took time but, as I mentioned, my forty-ish year marked a precarious new beginning which necessarily included the suffering that comes with the death of the old and the risk of the unknown.

Generally speaking, in my marriage and in my roles as a youth minister and religion teacher, I began to give voice to what I was beginning to discover, believe, and value through the experiences of those hints. I shared my spiritual perspective of the divine feminine and my disagreements with certain dogmas of the Church, all unacceptable to my husband and at odds with what others expected and insisted. Nevertheless, I no longer wanted to remain cautiously hushed or defensively avoidant, pleasing, or apologetic. Consequently, fear, conflict, judgment, and criticism assailed me in external and internal reality, sometimes shutting me down in a discordant tension of shame and guilt.

In time, the full rebellion manifested, and I made excruciatingly painful decisions for myself, the repercussions of which affected my adolescent sons, whom I deeply loved, for the four of us grieved the devoted, "ideal" mother I had identified with and they loved. How could a good mother consciously hurt her child by leaving? But they were no longer little boys, developmental separations well in process, and this was a different time for them and for me. I left my marriage of twenty-two years and moved into an apartment a few blocks away to stay involved with my sons, two still at home in high school; the oldest, eighteen, was away at college. I felt a gut-wrenching agony and hoped one day they would understand. The old mother/son relationships were dying, and the unknown relationship between each of us during this new reality was yet to be developed.

I also ended my work within Catholic institutions. I had already withdrawn from youth ministry programs when I began teaching. In the seniors' feminine spirituality course, I could no longer walk the razor's edge between attributing to God the Father a "feminine face" and ignoring the ancient Goddess myths and symbols of the divine feminine. I had been struggling, too, in the juniors' class about decision-making with the Church's standpoint on sexuality, artificial birth control, and its restraint from discussing forms of protection or prevention—other than abstinence. Both courses were, to me, especially important for young women to discuss at their ages. I realized that every religion, in their churches, synagogues, mosques, and schools, has a privilege and responsibility to lead and teach their congregations and students the beliefs, principles, and doctrines of that faith. But I could no longer remain within the confines of many Catholic proscriptions.

> *Your love has been so confined, so strangled, and you have kept yourself hidden.*

I found a job in a university research program and began graduate work in counseling psychology at Pacifica Graduate Institute. After the hints and rebellion, the dream of the Hanged One, the youth ministry work that had introduced me to Jung's *Psychological Types* (Jung, 1921/1971), the retreat meditation, and the feminine spirituality course that had invited my study of the work of female theologians, anthropologists, and Jungian analysts, as well as my lifelong interest in dreams and fairy tales, I'd decided I was interested in pursuing a path towards training to be a Jungian analyst. Thus, Pacifica's depth perspective for graduate work was important to me.

Pacifica required psychotherapy if enrolled in therapeutic coursework, so I began Jungian analysis with the only analyst in New Orleans at that time, a man who proved throughout the years to be the good "father" I had not experienced and a trusted ally in my newly developing relationship with my sons and with my inner masculine. Dreams symbolically conveying the tensions and decisions of my "world turned upside down" filled many hours—years. Analysis was crucial for me to confront unconscious realities, to risk the validity of my feelings, to trust and depend on the analytic relationship, and to discover the value in holding the tension of opposites. All this is to say, as the unending call of the complexes entered the fray, defenses continued their defending.

One of my earliest memories had been pivotal in hindering my willingness to speak up, creating a defense mechanism through an experience of shock and terror. My voice had been metaphorically crushed by my maternal grandfather's raging stranglehold around my grandmother's neck, choking her after she'd tearfully rebuked him for angrily breaking his breakfast dishes in the sink to display his discontent with the food she'd cooked and served. His hold wasn't fatal for my grandmother, who had stayed with him despite his infrequent volatile outbursts. However, I have wondered if, in his possessed state, he might have seriously hurt her had my aunt not run to him from our breakfast table screaming "Stop, Daddy!" And me? I just sat, spoon in hand, unable to move or to speak. True, I was only six years old. But my aunt was one year younger than I was. What did she have that I did not? A part of me must have thought, "That is what happens when you disagree or speak up."

At seven years old, one of only two years I'd attended Catholic school, I stood outside the church and waited in serious anticipation for our class to begin the procession for Mass. I was about to experience my first communion and receive the body of Christ on my tongue. My hands curved prayer-like around a small, white first communion missal as I heard the nun's anxious exclamations for us to get in line for the procession. Many of the girls were chattering excitedly, and the boys were pulling and pushing one another in distracted laughter. Despite this nun's unassuming, small, birdlike stature, her thickly layered white gown of authority swished distinctly around her ankles, and her long, black rosary beads announced her presence with that unmistakable clicking as she hurried along the undisciplined line of children clapping her hands for attention. Exasperated by what she must have encountered as a disrespectful lack of order, the nun stopped suddenly right beside me, raised both hands in clenched fists and angrily yelled, "Goddammit! Get in line!" Stunned by the curse and the image of her flushed, distorted face and clenched fists, I heard in the abrupt silence that followed somewhere within me, the sure sound of the cracking of holiness.

Fast forward to the dark night of secret, sacred vows. It was the night that the white knight on the white horse, dressed in my father's loose, short-sleeved white shirt and dark slacks, sloppily fell off his wounded steed, never to be hoisted up again. It was that same night that, in the associative mind of this nine-year-old, the aged, ineffective God, dressed in the white robes of eternity, fell off his royal throne, never to ascend it again.

I wasn't supposed to see this conflict, but bare feet are virtually silent on linoleum floors, and it took only one moment and one eye to peek around a corner to witness this obscenity that branded my memory. My mother's powerless anger railed vehemently, pointing its exhausted finger at my father as he slumped at our kitchen table, an aluminum rectangle on four legs and rounded at the corners, barely large enough to accommodate eight people, much less, at that time, ten; once again, his drowning eyes stared at her in that helpless, inebriated escape from the mistakes of his short twenty-eight years of life—which included one wife, eight children, and countless failures at keeping jobs of grandiose possibility.

Minutes later, strangely feeling not good enough and somehow blameworthy, I began, or some older-than-nine-year-old part of me began, to announce vows, three that I would unconsciously live by for quite some time. First, I would never subject my own children to the ugly anger and demeaning viciousness my mother desperately displayed toward my father. Second, I decisively denounced the God to whom I had prayed to help my parents stop arguing and my father to get better, the same God to whom those mothers of starving children in Africa must have prayed, all of us abandoned: no God of mine! And the (quite loaded) final vow: I would never need anyone again!

Three years in childhood, three formidable events, among others, suggesting to a child the danger of anger, and three vows that unconsciously confined my love: vows of protection, of defending the vulnerability of the little girl along with destroying her naturally naïve relationship with the divine. But vows can lose meaning, protection and defense are confronted by life, and conscious and unconscious realities, for better and worse, engage.

> *I have not remained so that you could give yourself away.*

But what has this to do with the dream of June 2008 and the crazed, knife-wielding killer, the Whinnying Woman, whose transformation, Self-image, mandala, and wisdom reprimanded and commanded more in the name of love? After fifteen years in analysis I had grown into myself—into the value of my feelings, into a more conscious relationship with the different complexes, shadow aspects, and animus images in my dreams and waking life. And the trials, the tormenting tensions of training, fueled the heat of individuation, inflaming the white-hot coals of an alchemical process that, like *her* fire, cooked snake.

I had gradually come out from hiding and suffered a layer of the emotions locked away by those early experiences and others that only conscious vulnerability can withstand. But there were times when I failed to recognize soon enough the cunning of the negative animus: He could interfere with an abduction here and a blindfold there. I learned this reality through painful experience. After having passed four of the five propaedeuticum exams and failing the dream exam in 2005, I had failed the retake the following year (April 2006). The first failure, in part, occurred when a menacing negative masculine entered the field, shocking me and the three female analysts on the committee with his contemptuous interference: This was one of the most humiliating and blatantly intrusive experiences of possession by this inner figure. In the retake, his presence was more subtle: I'd doubted and mistrusted my archetypal perspective of the dream and hid, instead, behind speaking with an intellectual interpretation using typology. This wasn't necessarily an incorrect interpretation, but it wasn't a genuinely grounded response in my experience in that moment. And worse, I failed to discuss the affect in the dream, always of deep significance, and, because the dream included an angry man with a knife who was threatening his brother, I especially needed to address the objective perspective.

Consequently, an analyst on the exam committee inquired about my neglect of the possible external reality of the dream image. After my response—that it hadn't occurred to me—she asked if I'd ever experienced that intensity of rage or danger. A sudden breath caught in my throat: A shocking realization and bodily sensation had claimed me and confronted me with yet another layer of that traumatic dynamic. I looked her in the eyes, defeated: "my grandfather." I'd thought I had done so much inner work regarding that stranglehold. The exam dream, itself, had constellated an unconscious field in which a dissociative defense had effectively cut off body and emotion and avoided the dangerous anger. I felt overwhelmed and exhausted at that time, and I wondered aloud: "I don't know if I can keep doing this." Their gentle response: "Go home. Don't open a book. We want you to come back next Spring for a retake."

> *She began drawing in the dirt—a cross of two equal lines and then four concentric circles on top of it. She did this slowly, placing the smallest, central circle at the point where the horizontal and vertical lines met and moved out from there.*

I was strengthened and challenged throughout that difficult year, in part by experiences, dreams, and symbols of the feminine and masculine offering consciousness of the deeper—sometimes beautiful, sometimes ugly—aspects of myself and of the archetypal nature of the realities of the psyche, of life. In one particular dream on October 21, 2006, six months before the retake, I was confronted by a ferocious bull, who disgusted me by lapping sewer water from an open manhole in the street and obstructed my escape by snorting fire. After waking and making an ink drawing of my head with the dark, piercing eyes of the bull, a snout spewing poisonous snot, and bared teeth resembling a shark's, I met him in active imagination:

> The snout of the bull spews fiery snot
> That poisons and burns
> And the sewer water
> Lapped up by an unknown desire

Sickens me
Dares me
Thwarts me
It is smart, cunning,
Obstructs my escape
And gores me in the gut
And the blood flows
And I taste it—
Then he tells me,
You cannot know something until you suffer it.
But how do I guard against hurting people?
You don't. You have to experience the repercussions.
Now, stand up and learn to handle the test.

I wanted to handle this test, to experience my fiery anger and the sewer water it drinks. It had gored me with a horn sharp as a knife and caused my blood to flow. Psyche feared such aggression from the rams. The repercussions were, for the most part, the suffering induced by my conscious experience of anger and what the effects of that suffering began to teach me about myself—of shadow aspects, of my narcissistic wound and my unconscious desire to be taken care of, of necessary separations, and of the stunted relating on which I'd relied, paled by the fear of the rams, or in my case, the bull. And it taught the recognition of others' shadows. My retake of the dream exam in April 2007 was a totally different experience, and I enjoyed it!

Throughout the rigors of analysis and training, the process of becoming conscious of the unconscious was colored by exquisite joy and heart-wrenching sorrow: success and failure, love and hate, courage and defense. My mantra, then, was from Jung: "The experience of the Self is always a defeat for the ego" (Jung, 1955-56/1970, para. 788). It is still true for me.

She pointed to the center circle. "I am here." Then she placed her finger on the outlying circle where the number two would be on the face of a clock. "And you are here."

Another of those defeats had occurred eight months after entering the "control stage"—Christmas Eve of 2007, when I had once again fallen into my lifelong caretaking habit for my mother and family. But what led to this critical nexus was an ever-increasing tension that felt unbearable in its domino effect: in 2004, two sons' deployment to the war in Iraq; in 2005, Hurricane Katrina—eight feet of water in my home, a beloved city in chaos, then relocation to Baton Rouge, which involved days of commuting each week to my practice, relocated to an unflooded area of New Orleans—and finally, my youngest, twenty-seven-year-old son's relocation with his love to another state. Then in 2006 came my analyst's illness and death, my middle son's return from Iraq, and his journey west in his own dark night of the soul. Such was the prelude to an explosion of anger hidden beneath fear and sorrow.

I wait for you to finally come.

That night of the gathering was somehow a pinnacle for the outbreak of a consuming fire growing in abject darkness, intense enough to char snake. (And, significant history here: My mother had bought and lived in my maternal grandparents' home.) After dinner and a few glasses of wine with the very large extended family and, subsequently, enclosed in the safety of a hotel room, I experienced an other-worldly rage, witnessed by my brother and closest friend, that, in my intoxicated state, had surfaced only once before: In 1993, in spite of mediation, I had to make a decision regarding my husband's adamant demand against speaking about spirituality or sexuality with my sons in order to share custody. At that time, alone (and very sober) in my apartment, and infuriated by his continued control, I'd become what felt like a wild thing, wanting to destroy everything around me, including the stacks of art honoring my dreams. Fortunately, I did not destroy the art, and, because of one son's entreaty to choose them, I did agree to my husband's demand. I just had to find a way that *that* sacrifice would not destroy *me*.

Erinys

Loosened on this night by a Dionysian influence of import, I had witnesses who contained and patiently held the crazed, acerbic rage unleashed in that hotel room. I did not recognize my guttural, malevolent growl: "I am so through with you!

We are finished." The next day, after the hours' drive home, I felt mortified and defeated, yet the rage and its unapologetic possession left me determined to seek its purpose. I used acrylic pastels to create the horrifying feeling tone of the experience—to relate to what its image might be. What took form on the blank paper was a dark feminine image, the head of a female enraged. She looked and felt like what I'd imagined to be an Erinys (the "Erinys" drawing)! I had heard of these mythic creatures and knew vaguely, at that time, of their fury for Orestes's murder of his mother Clytemnestra.

"I am through with you": the vestiges of the old role of mothering and caretaking while unconsciously abandoning myself. "We are finished": the controlling, negative inner masculine with which I had been struggling in the projections onto my husband, the Church, and that particular male analyst. Easier said than done, but I was determined: The Whinnying Woman came as a killer with a knife months after those proclamations.

Now, it begins.

The heat of training had increased in this control stage: My case colloquium facilitator and group, case supervisors, and my thesis and cases committees had been established. I was not concerned with organizing my thesis, for I'd been writing about "The Kiss" for years from different perspectives in my formal papers for the New Orleans training seminars.

My cases committee was a different story, in part because the male analyst chosen as one of the committee members had been on committees for my interviews and exams, including the dream exam I'd failed in 2006. This analyst had received my negative animus projection for a few years, and now he had been placed on my cases committee. Since I had felt more grounded in myself, and since this man had served on the dream exam I'd just passed, in which the negative masculine did not interfere, I felt cautious but open to this ironic challenge.

Now it begins—as I'd mentioned earlier, never could I have imagined the anguish and work necessary to relate to this negative animus over the next two years. I often felt "crazy," delusional, and assailed by critical thoughts. The affects and consciousness reverberating within those circles of the Self were both strengthening and challenging. I was developing a taste for charred snake.

I realized that my feelings of fear and insecurity had constellated the early trauma and the image of a choked voice writing the cases. Yet relating to another little girl in a compensatory dream on October 25, 2008, was part of the healing for the wounded child and the strangled love:

> *I am in a school cafeteria. There is a little girl here that must be new, so I go to her and take her to the person behind the counter to see about getting her some food. There is some problem, and I don't think she gets any. I talk to her; she tells me her name is Grace, and she reaches for the necklace she is wearing—a delicate gold chain that has a ceramic ornament hanging from it. The hanging piece is a little girl, like herself, skipping. It is painted in pastel colors and the little girl is smiling, and so is Grace. She flicks the ornament with her finger, and it looks as though the legs are skipping.*

To meet Grace! Where a gold chain like this might often carry a tiny crucifix or cross, her ornament was painted in the pastel colors of the wave of light that had formed twenty years earlier at the retreat as my image of the "feminine face" of God: Back then, the soft voice from the wave told me her name was Lily. These pastel colors were also the colors of the cumulus clouds of that first "Hanged One" dream, on which were printed "God" and "unity." And now Grace wore the colors on an emblem of a smiling little girl in joyful play. For me, she symbolized the grace of the ongoing relationship with the divine feminine and my own feminine self. These colors of the rainbow, the bridge between heaven and earth, had appeared as a living symbol in different forms at pivotal moments in my life. And, although I had no idea about the meaning, the words "God" and "unity" of that numinous first dream seemed to invite a divine union—masculine and feminine, heaven and earth. And since I had steeped myself in the masculine God, the feminine Goddess had emerged and, yes, turned my world upside down.

Throughout this time the animus had appeared in dreams in its negative and positive aspects: unknown masculine figures who threatened or destroyed along with others that supported and encouraged. The images, characteristics, and dynamics of this archetype would become even more crucial, because on February 1, 2009, my committee chair called to tell me the vote for permission for me to take the exam was two to one, and it was up to me whether or not to take it. Their feedback stated my "maternal analytic stance" was solid, but they wanted to see more of my "paternal, penetrating stance."

In response to this news, a dream on February 3rd, reminiscent of the Whinnying Woman with her knife, depicted a masculine focus on love and the purpose of his knife:

> *I am sitting with my case colloquium leader, his wife, and another woman. He is staring as if remembering or seeing something: "It's about God. It is all about love." He speaks with such reverence, and I am deeply moved. I wake up.*
>
> *I go back to sleep and dream I am in the backseat of a car. I want to write down the dream I'd just had. An unknown man gets in the back seat—tall, with*

> *grayish hair. He gives me a piece of paper and an X-Acto knife to write down the dream. I do this and notice the man must have written something, because there are letters cut out on the other side of where I'm writing.*
> *Then, I'm in a house, and he comes in and says, "I know you are a candidate. What exams are you taking?" I tell him I'm taking the final exams. He responds, "I will always vote against you."*

I felt so defeated, and yet unwilling to just accept his emphatic rejection. His voice had the tone and judgment of the masculine who interfered in that first dream exam—again, he was here! I went back into this dream and decided to speak with him about this in an active imagination. In our dialogue he'd pointed out what he'd thought were huge mistakes I'd made in life, including hurting my sons, and scoffed that I needed to be "perfect" and was, instead, "weak." My responses were not defensive but grounded in genuine experience and feelings, acknowledging my developing consciousness, inquiring about his insistence on perfection, and questioning its possibility in life. In my conscious effort to relate to him, I bought an X-Acto knife in a pencil shape and did what he'd directed—I "wrote" the dream on a sheet of paper, which was difficult to do. Dreams of the threatening masculine persisted, sometimes confronted by positive masculine figures, and many dialogues with the "X-Acto Man" continued, each diminishing in opposition and growing in alliance. I came to an understanding of the kind of love the case colloquium analyst of that dream meant, the kind of love the Erinys demanded and the Whinnying Woman released, the kind of love I'd learned to give to and receive from the animus. With practice writing that dream on sheets of paper, I discovered the X-Acto knife's purpose—of applying only a certain amount of pressure, of being exact, precise in my thoughts and focus. This aspect, I'd determined, was part of the paternal stance the male analyst wanted to see written in my cases, which I had mistakenly thought was evident. Although my relationship with the "X-Acto Man" had begun with animosity, it had developed into one of respect and love. It had been a very long and mysterious process in which we'd both been transformed. I'd honored us with an ink drawing of a black and white snake entitled "Love Exactly" (the "Love Exactly" image).

Love Exactly

Six weeks later the qualities of my new, conscious feminine ground and his transformed spirit, his positive Logos, united to produce a vibrant baby girl, a numinous "moon-flower tree," and a unanimous pass on both exams. My thesis committee of three sealed my thesis with a kiss—all at once, they kissed me, one on each cheek and one on my forehead. I carried that kiss with me into the cases exam, along with Lily, the Whinnying Woman, the X-Acto Man, and Grace (the image "The Aliveness of Grace and Me")—as well as the love and support of so many in my life.

The Aliveness of Grace and Me

The wounds of my childhood and the vows of innocence had been defended, suffered, and loved into consciousness. It was not a linear path of cognitive knowing, but a circular path of living down into its emotional turmoil and its impact on my life. With a new vow of relatedness to the unconscious realities of the psyche, I continued the journey into and with parts of myself.

The danger of anger, at one time feared, had now become necessity: Hurting others was unavoidable, and hurting myself possible, but anger's instinctual energy found and continues to discover its assertive purpose for the growth of consciousness. The Erinys of that Christmas Eve? I'd learned her mythic fury was in defense of the mother, whether mother was right or wrong. What was invaluable for me was to experience the depth and power of that rage and to work with its declarations and process its purpose in analysis and active imagination for some time afterward. And the Whinnying Woman? I had read Jung's *Symbols of Transformation* (Jung, 1952/1967) and related her, then, to the mother, the body, and the horse as a symbol of instinctual life. What I had not known until writing this story, was that Demeter, the mother goddess, was known as a horse-headed goddess. Her mythic story, in brief, told of her grieving search for her abducted daughter, Persephone. Poseidon pursued her during her agony, and Demeter tried to escape him by becoming a mare and joining a herd of steeds. Poseidon discovered the trick and transformed into a stallion and coupled with Demeter. Thus, she was known as the horse-headed goddess. As a result of Poseidon's over-powering her, this "wrathful goddess turned into Erinys, the goddess of anger, and was actually called Demeter Erinys until she washed away her anger in a river ..." (Kerényi, 1980, p. 185). Yes, my Erinys's rage called forth, only months later, the crazed Whinnying Woman I'd sketched with a horse head, amplified now by Demeter Erinys. No longer had I neglected her fury within, and my desire to finally relate to her and meet her gaze was a transformational experience. She had come to give me more. Her knife was instrumental in killing off an old attitude of the masculine and feminine I had adopted, and it was useful in preparing bite-sized pieces of fire-roasted snake. That knife remains in reach.

"No God of mine!" Separation from this God, announced in a child's state of emotional pain and shattered beliefs, left me with a spiritual wound that seemed to ooze and pulsate deep within, surfacing periodically in remnants of feelings and thoughts. However, this vow turned out to be true in its hidden mystery. The childish perception of the God who answers all prayers had to change, and the one-sidedness of my adult perspective of the divine Father/Son, although life-giving in many ways, left an unconscious longing for His counterpart. Dreams and Jungian analysis and training had been invaluable in deepening the image of divinity, which includes for a woman the divine Mother/Daughter, the Kore.

My experience of the Whinnying Woman and the mandala identified her unmistakable place in the center of my wholeness, my Self, and her message of my strangled love gave me more of that wholeness. She came at a time when I would learn the significance and challenge of that message in relation, especially, to the animus. And I am grateful, so grateful. Through her I also became more conscious of the interplay of the archetypes and the invitation by my complexes to relate to my emotional depths and spiritual life. Introduced to the archetype in my dream of the "Hanged One" before I even knew the word, I have become very conscious of the aw-ful and awe-some psychic powers they carry and deliver. To read about them is one thing, and to relate to them is quite another.

The nun's "Goddammit, get in line" and my grandfather's "Goddammit, get in here" cracked like thunder, each at different times but, nonetheless, so very declarative in expectation. This god-damning judgment from my negative animus was characteristic of that spirit as he wielded his agency of thoughts and destruction.

Had I not desired the alchemical gold from this masculine figure and his X-Acto knife in the dream, I may have missed another healing experience of the transformative energy of Eros.

And my little girl's final vow, "I would never need anyone again!"? We learned it was not true: She needed me, and I needed to relate to her. My training in love has insisted on my relating to the unconscious realities of my inner world. This consciousness of love's tensions and manifestations and, especially, its archetypal images and complexities has, indeed, given me more. She has given me more. He has given me more. And the training in love—it begins again and again.

The Healing of Medusa: A Dream Journey

Barbara Friedman

I have approached this work with a sacred attitude. I ask that you join me to embark on a symbolic story of healing told through dreams, myths, and fairy tales. At the heart of the story is love. Love, as I've come to believe, is the middle way that both Carl Jung and the Buddha were teaching. Jung's individuation process and the Buddha's enlightenment are both spiritual *experiences* based on love. Rilke describes these experiences beautifully:

> *For they are the moments when something new has entered into us, something unknown; our feelings grow mute in shy perplexity, everything in us withdraws, a stillness comes, and the new, which no one knows, stands in the midst of it and is silent. (Rilke, 1929/2021, pp. 65-66)*

I am eighty years old. In looking back at my life, as people tend to do at my age, I have found it profoundly meaningful and healing to remember my journey through images from my most memorable dreams and their archetypal amplifications depicted in myths and fairy tales. The simple recounting of events: I got married; I went to grad school; I had a career; I had kids; I got divorced. Yet these events somehow fail to get to the heart of the matter, whereas exploring my dreamscapes and their associations illuminated my inner spiritual journey. This personal process has also connected me to the struggles we all face as humans and the powerful archetypal forces that influence us.

I, like most people, have sometimes felt lost in my life, like I'd made the wrong turn. When I finally made a conscious effort to confront the unconscious defenses my ego put forward to protect me, I realized that I was not lost, because the process is the path. Through this understanding, I have largely been able to forgive myself and, subsequently, others. I used to think forgiveness was just another burden given to the victim, but I've come to learn it is gifted to us through love and compassion.

I hope the images I share convey the otherworldly energy of archetypes: how they pulled me this way and that; how I became entangled like a tumbleweed in collective conditioning and rolled along, turning in directions I thought were my choices but weren't; how I unknowingly acted out their wills. Then, with the help of my own analysis and my training as a Jungian psychoanalyst, I learned that these images, conjured by my unconscious, offered me an eagle's eye view of my life. My haunting dreams, permeated with myths and fairy tales, were showing me that I was walking a labyrinth where all paths eventually led to the center. No matter how lost or dizzy from the many twists and turns, I was on my way.

It's a privilege to share my story, and I hope it might inspire you to remember and examine your own. It's the only method I've found to understand what I've been up against and, more importantly, to release my unkind judgements of myself and, thus, of others. Jesus's words echo: "Father, forgive them for they know not what they do" (King James Bible, Luke 23:34).

I am risking being transparent and vulnerable in my desire to share the wisdom of Lao Tzu's message in the *Tao Te Ching*:

I have just three things to teach:
simplicity, patience, compassion.
These three are your greatest treasures.
Simple in actions and in thoughts,
you return to the source of being.
Patient with both friends and enemies,
you accord with the way things are.
Compassionate toward yourself,
you reconcile all beings in the world.
(Lao Tzu, 1988/2006, verse 67)

He wrote this about 2,400 years ago, and, as far as I can tell, it's still true.

My children are in danger

Dream: My Children Are in Danger

A vivid nightmare. Even now, forty years later, its effect is still chilling. In the dream I'm on a hill overlooking my house. My children are trapped inside by ruthless men. The children are in grave danger. I'm frozen, helpless.

At the time I had this dream, I was volunteering at a free medical clinic in Cleveland, Ohio, and teaching women to examine their breasts for cancer. I remember having the thought that I shouldn't be teaching this and not practicing it myself. So, one day in the shower, I examined my own breasts—very intimate probing, feeling for a small defined lump. I still hate the word lump! And there it was—a tiny round lump in my left breast. It was not like anything else I'd felt, and I knew it was trouble.

Luckily, I was a privileged white girl who had medical insurance and an OB-GYN I trusted. He did a needle biopsy in his office. I was there but kind of not there, a skill I learned to employ in childhood. Later that week, I was sitting at my desk between client sessions when the doctor called. He asked, "Do you really want the results over the phone?" I told him I didn't want to wait, for I knew he wouldn't have asked *that* question if it was good news. Yes, I had breast cancer. This hit me like a charge from a stun gun. If I thought I was frozen in the dream—this was a new level of freeze.

I'm a researcher by nature, and I uncovered the fact that one out of every four women in my community had been struck with breast cancer. What the fuck was going on?!

Back then, I intuitively understood that something moved me—call it intuition—to do the self-exam. And that self-exam literally saved my life. My dream had been trying to warn me. I had missed the initial warning, and I didn't want that to happen again. I wondered who could help me unravel the symbolism?

Vocatta's house

Dream: Vocatta's House—The Dream Whisperer

My therapist friends told me about a dream whisperer, a Jungian analyst named Vocatta. She lived and worked in an old Victorian house with ancient pots, some cracked, filled with overgrown plants and placed on the steps leading up to a vine-covered door. It was clearly the house of a good witch.

The name Vocatta, which means *vocation*, was given to her in a ritual by a shaman rabbi in California in the 1970s. Of course, where and when else! Vocatta created a sacred space where conscious and unconscious could speak to each other safely, and thus transformation could occur. She was fluent in the language of symbol and knew how to help me translate the meaning of my dreams. It was a reciprocal process between the dreams, my analyst and me. We explored my associations and the realm of the archetypes, the overarching patterns that form our experiences here in middle earth, the mortal realm. Our view of reality is refracted through conditioning by these forces, and we are often held hostage to it. With time and struggle, Vocatta helped me work to be free of these conditioned patterns.

During my first visit we sat in faded Victorian chairs on her shabby-chic sun porch. Before we looked at my nightmare, she said, "Can you recall the very first dream you remember from childhood? It may illuminate the purpose of our work together."

Gracemount Elementa

Dream: Gracemount Elementary School

This is the earliest dream I can recall. In the dream I'm at my elementary school and am sent to the old building to bring a kindergarten boy to the principal's office in the new building. I feel honored to be given this mission.

There really was an old wooden building and a new brick building at my elementary school. And I can picture myself walking down the corridor in the old building, holding the hand of a small, dark-haired boy, feeling protective. Did this event really happen? Fantasy and reality warp. Vocatta was a very direct and intuitive person. She remarked, "Bringing an undeveloped masculine energy to a new principle is your life's journey."

The Minoan Snake Goddess

Dream: The Minoan Snake Goddess

The next dream I remember featured a young woman from an ancient culture. Snakes coil around her proudly raised arms. She is upright, strong, safe, and independent.

Vocatta was taken with the figure and shared the myth about this snake-woman figure. In the ancient Minoan civilization, she told me, the snake woman was powerful, revered. Those snakes, held high in her outstretched arms, were venerated for their connection to the earth—the ground of being—and for their ability to transform as they shed their old skin for a new one. This image, she said, was from a time when women were honored, from 3000–1100 B.C.E. (George, 1986).

Synchronistically, the snake goddess figure invaded my waking life, too. Wandering through The British Museum in London, I did a double take. There, in a glass case, stood a small statue of this proud lady. She was magnetic! I felt like I was under her spell.

Dream: The Slaying of Medusa

Adding to these phenomenal events, not long after The British Museum visit, I dream of the slaying of Medusa by the hero Perseus. In the dream he appears, brandishing the goddess Athena's protective shield and flying on the borrowed wings of the god Hermes. Medusa lies dead, decapitated, limbs akimbo and blood flowing everywhere. Terrified, angry snakes slither in every direction.

Why were Athena, the father god Zeus's daughter, and Hermes, the boundary-crossing god of communication, aiding in the slaying of Medusa? A field of violent energy was taking form in my psyche. I felt deeply emotional and more than a little freaked

Slaying of Medusa

out. The images seemed to have a purpose—trying to show me something. Who was talking to me? How could I explain this?

As I said, I'm a researcher. I couldn't let this go.

I sought out feminist interpretations of the myth of Medusa, which these scholars revised from the traditional patriarchal versions that were, at the time, widely accepted. They suggested that the myth describes a transitional historical time in which patriarchal forces ravaged goddess-worshiping civilizations in brutal battles. Many patriarchal traditions include a version of the Medusa story: The Old Testament Book of Psalms describes Yahweh's victory over the cosmic sea serpent, Leviathan (New Revised Standard Bible, Catholic Edition, 1990, Psalm 74:14). In the Vedic tradition of India, there is the story of King Indra's victory over the cosmic serpent, Vitra (Campbell, 1976).

And according to Greek mythology, after the gods of the Greek pantheon defeated the great earth goddess, they divided up the spoils of victory: Poseidon took the sea, Zeus, the heavens, and Hades, the underworld. This was the first of many colonizations to follow this androcentric pattern.

According to those feminist historians, the violence of the patriarchal takeover was indefensible. And the way the followers of the new patriarchal gods used power to dominate had devastating effects which can still be felt today. The patriarchal coup vanquished a matriarchal culture which, according to the feminist anthropological and archeological studies, did not comprehend the idea of domination and control. According to these investigators, matriarchal civilizations were based on a reverence for nature, harmony, and equality. Power was more thought of in terms of responsibility toward others rather than domination over others (Eisler, 1987, pp. 29–41; Gimbutas, 2001).

And yet, it is also true that these matriarchal civilizations became violent, and they castrated men. This was a hint of a more complicated story which I dismissed at that time. I now, however, see my avoidance of that reality as a defense.

I also discovered a surprising account of Medusa in a book from the *Monsters of Mythology* series, *Medusa* by Bernard Evslin (1987). In Evslin's re-telling of the myth, Medusa's mother, Ceto, was the goddess of the sea. Medusa's father, Phorcys, lived folded into Ceto's voluminous skin. This description implied the matriarchal domination and minimization of men, an historical complication which, as I mentioned, I had defensively avoided. Medusa was the only human-looking offspring born of this couple. She was beautiful, with flowing coils of tawny golden hair, whereas her sisters were described as gorgons, ugly monsters. Medusa was amphibious, at home swimming in the sea and walking on the land. She represented the archetypal transitional character, depicting a time when consciousness rose out of the sea of the unconscious.

When Poseidon claimed power, planting his trident like a flag on the seafloor, he arranged for a race to be held among the sea nymphs, planning to take the winner for himself: a perpetrator grooming his prey. He asked the cyclops Brontes to forge a necklace out of pearls and gold from the sea, which he would give to the nymph he chose. It's important to note that the goddess Athena, who had emerged from her father Zeus's head after he swallowed her pregnant mother Metis, witnessed the necklace being forged. She was consumed with envy because of the loss of her mother and the theft of feminine power by Zeus. Burning with resentment, she was determined that the necklace and, symbolically, the jewels of the lost feminine would be hers.

Before the race had begun, Poseidon saw Medusa poised on a rock; her coils of golden hair parted to reveal her beautiful breasts. He wanted her. He gave her the necklace which Brontes had forged and, with patriarchal entitlement, he raped her. He assumed she was his property, the first trophy wife.

However, Medusa was not aware of the new rules of possession and ownership. When she later saw a fisher-lad drowning in the sea, she followed her natural instincts and saved his life. Then, holding him to her, she comforted and loved him. Poseidon was enraged. She was his property.

The myth goes on to say that when the fisher-lad reclaimed his boat and returned to the sea, the world had changed. Athena, seared with envy, had turned Medusa's hair to snakes. When the lad saw them, instead of a symbol of earthbound, feminine energy, he perceived them through the new patriarchal lens as evil and dangerous. He'd lost his connection to his experience of the healing instinctual energy of the transformational feminine, and he was petrified. He turned to stone and sank to the bottom of the sea, depicting how men's fear of women could turn them stone cold—separated from the feminine relational source.

Horrified, shamed, and grief-stricken by Poseidon's rape and the fisher-lad's reaction and demise, Medusa now viewed herself as ugly, so ugly that those who saw her turned to stone. She tore off the necklace, which Athena triumphantly caught. Medusa fled to the farthest reaches of the sea, where she became an exile, feared by all men. Her first trauma response was flight. Over time, she became cold-hearted; she froze, her second trauma response. Her third trauma response was to fight back, a bitter woman filled with the rage that often accompanies shame. She became an *angry* exile who enjoyed the power of terrifying men and turning them to stone. I recognized Medusa's trauma responses in myself and connected with her on a personal level. I, too, could be cold and angry, passive-aggressively turning men to stone, even the men whom I begged to love me.

Vocatta helped me link my personal experiences to the transpersonal or archetypal meaning of this myth. She explained myths as collective representations expressing universal truths about the culture and offering meaning to individual struggles. On a personal level, these myths describe the aggressive masculine takeover within the psyches of individual women and their trauma responses, which are pathologized. That struck a chord with me: I could be ingratiating and adaptable, not recognizing mistreatment. Then I would become resentful and angry, like Medusa was. I could only express my resentment passively because of a fear of abandonment. I was gaining a new perspective on my behavior.

WTF

Dream: WTF?

In the next related dream, the snakes crawl away from the defeated and angry goddess, who screams, "What the fuck?"

I was relieved to realize my issues, my shame and anger, had a known and long history related to internalized misogyny. I felt less isolated, but I also felt destabilized, like the plates of the earth were moving under me. I became conscious that the inherent shame and rage I had turned against myself came from internalizing the patriarchal fear and hatred of the feminine.

My dreams and the feminist interpretations of these mythical stories opened me to the long history of the patriarchy's oppression of women. External oppression was quickly followed by internal oppression—within my own psyche—where women become perpetrators against ourselves. I did not like this! So, like a black panther, I started dressing in black, donned a black beret, and became an angry feminist bitch!

I was energized and no longer frozen. I fought for abortion rights. My friends and I started an illegal hotline on the third floor of my friend's duplex to help women who wanted abortions travel to New York. I was pretty sure the FBI was following me. I taught women to do breast self-exams at the free clinic. I stood up for myself with partners and friends. "Don't mess with me!" was my attitude. My snakes were hissing.

When I researched the classical interpretation of the Medusa myth, I was enraged to discover the sexist validation of the atrocities against womankind. For example, Joseph Campbell held that inherent to the process of becoming conscious is the fight for free will and "a self-moving destiny over any earthbound serpent destiny" (Campbell, 1976, p. 24). He depicted the dawning of the light of ego consciousness coming out of the darkness of the maternal sea of the unconscious. Historians with that patriarchal lens agreed and considered the violent ending of the goddess-worshiping civilizations to be a developmental milestone for the culture and the individual.

These historians maintained that, to the rising masculine consciousness, the earth goddess or the feminine (and, in conflating gender and sex, women in general) are a source of danger, a terrifying enemy. When faced with her potent power, a man can become catatonic with fear, unable to move forward in his evolutionary path, just as the fisher-lad stood frozen with fear when he gazed at Medusa. The mission of the developing ego is to free itself, even through violent means, from the archaic feminine, which is understood to be a necessary step in the development of a more rational and superior humanity.

I believed the feminine gender in general and individual women themselves had been wounded and were in grave danger. On the collective level, the earth had been (and is being) ravaged—the nurturing gifts of the great mother squandered and destroyed. On a very personal and intimate level, I felt ravaged, without connection to instincts that would have allowed me to protect and nurture myself and my children. My breast cancer seemed to me a physical manifestation of this wounding.

I concluded that this was the meaning of the original nightmare I had brought to Vocatta. My inner child and my actual children were trapped by the negative masculine. That trauma had immobilized me at the time, even though I knew, as a history major in undergrad, that history can be told from many perspectives. At this point, I chose the radical feminist revisionist version. Anger felt active and much more alive than the urge to flee or freeze. Anger is often a necessary step toward self-agency.

Negative animus

Dream: Negative Animus

In the next major dream of the series, I am locked in a room with a sadistic man. He is lounging in an oversized chair with a pistol in his hand—casual, cool. His posture says, "I can do whatever I want to you, and you won't be able to do a thing about it." He will take his time. He is reveling in his power and feeling erotic pleasure from my fear and helplessness. I wake up terrified, unable to sleep, trapped again.

This man was a Bluebeard type. In the fairy tale, Bluebeard murdered his many wives. Because she was curious and not frozen, his last wife unlocked a forbidden door and found their skeletons. She realized she would soon meet the same fate. Marie-Louise von Franz, one of Jung's most formidable protégés, characterized Bluebeard as the darkest, most diabolical aspect of the patriarchy and the negative masculine in a woman's psyche. He was a force that cut a woman off from life, and he represented the abuse of power: power over a woman and erotic sadomasochism. She insisted there was nothing transformative about this traumatic situation. The woman must be rescued and flee (von Franz, 1974, p. 169).

In the fairy tale *Bluebeard*, the last wife's brothers came to rescue her on horseback. The hoofbeats of the positive masculine connected her to her power. Panicked, I realized that in my personal life I was waiting for a hero to appear on his trusty steed and rescue me from harmful relationships both in my marriage and within my own psyche. Where was my horse? Where were my brothers? Who was going to rescue me? I was longing for an idealized rescuer in an idealized world, a very passive position and a reflexive one for me—the angry victim (West, 2016, p. 130).

Dream: Two Chalices of My Own Blood

In a startling dream, an animated and feminine voice commanded, "You must drink two chalices of your own blood!"

In a Greek myth, Athena gave to Asclepius, the wounded god of healing, two vials of Medusa's blood. According to the tale, the blood from Medusa's left vein would destroy and the blood from the right vein would cure. As both vials were essential to Asclepius, they symbolized the balance needed in my own healing journey (Downing, 1990).

Two chalices of my own blood

The Blood From Her Left Vein Will Destroy

I had been working with Vocatta for about five years by now and was in training to become a Jungian analyst. I was finally ready to swallow the truth serum from Medusa's left vein. I realized that I had already taken the first sip of the power in Medusa's red blood when I had tasted the rage of the shamed and exiled feminine. But now I was sucked into the darkest depths of the terrorized, rejected, ostracized feminine in both subtle and blatant ways.

I reflected on how I had been mistreated, underestimated, belittled, ignored, and reduced, how I had internalized many negative and often devastating messages about myself, resulting in feeling powerless, passive, and accommodating. All that I had believed had kept me safe, including my mantle of sweetness and crown of self-sacrifice, was destroyed at the gates to this underworld (Perera, 1981). Again, I wanted to fight, to feel assertive, to be aggressive in pursuit of my own needs. No one in my life liked it. No one said, "How brave! Good for you! You go girl!" To the contrary, others wanted the codependent friend, colleague, or partner they had relied on. Only my analyst congratulated me. And she held, contained, and accepted these feelings and their necessary repercussions.

The Blood From Her Right Vein Will Heal

In the depths of this dark place, I cried every morning for a year as I walked my golden retriever. I gradually released my relentless hope for rescue, that a man would come to love me enough to make up for my narcissistic father, or that I would receive the mirroring that my mother couldn't give me. Each of them had been wounded by the patriarchy. I realized that I had idealized men and then hated them for my disappointment, that I blamed my mother for her inability to protect me or herself, and that my self-righteous anger, as well as a myriad of other defenses, came from the inflation I needed to protect myself from experiencing the raw helplessness, dependency, and vulnerability that were a natural part of life.

I sobbed as I confronted my complicity in this dynamic and the complicated historical wounding of my family. I began to understand that, although in many ways I had been a victim, I had identified with this role and was therefore splitting off the perpetrator. Slowly I began to understand my feelings of powerlessness and helplessness. A split-off part of my own psyche had internalized the perpetrator and become self-destructive. I felt physically and mentally awful.

I felt such dismay about how I'd lived—lost in my defenses. But I also felt the preciousness of life and the hope that there was a way out of my suffering. I intuitively knew that facing vulnerability and pain—staring Medusa in the eye—was necessary for healing. Breaking this pattern of behavior was like atomic fission—energy was released.

I dropped the ball

Dream: I Dropped the Ball

My young son and I are playing ball. I miss the catch, and the ball falls off a cliff into a ravine. I say, "Oh well, whatever." But I should care; I've lost the ball! I've lost track of my path, of nurturing myself and my children. "I don't care" is a "collapse" trauma response: I give up; I have no power. "I don't care" is another of my conditioned defenses to avoid the pain and grief for what I had lost by negating my needs, desires, and beliefs. Buddhist teaching says apathy is the "near enemy" to caring; reactivity is the "close enemy."

There is a fairy tale called *The Frog Prince* (Grimm, 2013). In the tale a young princess was playing on the castle grounds with her golden ball. She tossed it and rolled it in the lush grasses. After a time, the princess threw the ball up so high that she missed catching it, and the ball rolled along the ground until it fell into a swampy ravine. The princess bewailed her loss and cried, "If I could only have my ball, I would give all my jewels and wealth." After a time, a frog appeared with the ball in his slimy mouth. He told her, "If you take me home, sleep with me in your gilded and sweet-smelling bed, and kiss me with love, I will return the ball."

Recalling the frog prince story as I worked with my dream, I got the gist of the message. By this point in my Jungian training and the work with Vocatta, I was getting good at the symbolizing thing. It was clear, I must kiss the inner frog, the slimy creature who I thought was beneath me and projected onto others, especially men, and particularly my partner. I needed to give up my inflated self-righteousness, the isolated palace and the princess thing. The tale insisted I must kiss him *because* I had learned how to love him. That meant no performance: authenticity. That meant becoming intimate with the ugliest parts of myself that, like the frog who had crawled out of the swamp, needed to be loved. I had to open my closed heart to the misogynistic parts of myself that had penetrated my psyche. That meant no more splitting.

As my defenses began to fray, my pain and vulnerability confronted me. I started to feel compassion for my own suffering. I began to care for myself. Oh, how I cared! I could feel the depth of my pain, because I understood the predicament I had faced, and *that* understanding opened my heart to self-love. I discovered that love is compassionate understanding while refusing to surrender to abuse. This compassion didn't come from me or belong to me. It was given to me. I held my nose and took another long swig from the healing chalice of grief. Ughh! How many unconscious decisions I'd made! I tasted how I had endangered myself and hurt others. Conscious grief is healing.

In the fairy tale, when the princess lived in intimacy with the frog and discovered she genuinely loved him, he turned into a prince, of course. Here is the first appearance of the positive masculine. I had to discover a more positive and nuanced internal and external relationship with the masculine. Like my original childhood dream had predicted, I needed to bring the masculine from the archaic misogynistic place it lived to a new principle. I, like Medusa and Bluebeard's wives, had been locked in the stubborn belief that I was a victim. This view had held me captive. I needed to liberate myself from this fixed perspective. But this independence from my old stance and reality demanded substantial sacrifice. I saw it was up to me. The old structure, supported by my passively waiting to be saved and angrily fighting to defeat, must be sacrificed for a new one. Towers must topple; relationships must change. This process was one of great loss and grieving. Even fantasies must be grieved.

The raft

Dream: The Raft

Years later, when I am in my late 60s and working with a different analyst, I dream that I'm on a raft going across a river with my horse on the way to Dharamshala. This is where the Dalai Lama fled for safety from Chinese repression.

By now my children were grown and on their own, and I was finally ready to leave my 33-year marriage. I had the profound knowledge that if I stayed in that unhappy union, internally and externally, I'd literally get sick and die, maybe experience a recurrence of cancer. People thought I was crazy, a 63-year-old woman moving to a new town. But I was fleeing for my own survival. I must be my own brothers coming to save myself. It was when I was about to leave the city for the last time that I had this dream.

Only later, when I found my Buddhist teachers in the new city, did I discover the Raft Sutta (written teachings). In the Alagaddūpama Sutta, the Buddha compares his teaching to a raft. The raft, he says, is for the purpose of crossing over, not for the purpose of holding onto. You let it go when you have reached the other shore, having fully integrated the teachings (Alagaddūpama Sutta, 1995, p. 228).

However, the monk Thanissaro explains that, although it's true that the raft of the noble eightfold path of Buddhism is abandoned on reaching the other shore, you still must hold on to it while crossing the river (Alagaddūpama Sutta, 2004). Otherwise, you'll be swept downstream. Buddhist teachings have served as my raft to liberation from my reactive conditioned responses.

Dream: Buddhist Precepts and Transmission

I dreamed a Buddhist teacher gave me dharma transmission, the passing down of authentic spiritual wisdom from teacher to student.

In my new city, along with a Buddhist teacher, I found many Buddhist temples and joined a Korean Zen *sangha* (group). I eventually took precepts, Buddhist vows, and I was given the name "Jeonbeop," which means the true dhamma, i.e., wholesome teachings. Yet, I followed the path somewhat sluggishly. I understood it, but I wasn't really in it with two feet. Several years later, I was introduced to a Vipassana sangha and a teacher. I liked this particular Buddhist path because it was very psychological;

Buddhist precepts

however, I also followed it halfheartedly. The venerable teacher noticed: "You're very adaptable, aren't you?"

I proudly acknowledge: "Yes."

He ruthlessly responds: "We call that sloth and torpor."

At first, I was shocked and offended, but then I saw the truth. I set the intention to become steadfast in my commitment to the path. I found the promise of space and freedom was true when I realized the four noble truths. *Duhkha* or sorrow exists, that's true. *Anicha*, that nothing is permanent, is obviously true. *Anata*, that no permanent self exists, is true. Then the fourth, that suffering you create yourself can end when you realize there is nothing to cling to and you let go, must also be true.

I saw the wheel of *samsara*, the pain and suffering caused by delusions—of dependent origination—from this, follows that—and how it spins us round and round, repeating old patterns that don't work. There was nothing to do but let go and step out of the wheel. I let go of clinging to the projected, inflated belief that I would find a way to make up for all that was lost or that I never had. I was able to stay open to pain and suffering because they are a natural part of life. I saw that not doing so obstructed accepting things as they are.

Dream: The Burning Ship

I dream of a burning sailing ship surrounded by wild waves.

Thank God for my Buddhist studies. Buddhism, by the way, has no God archetype unless you count emptiness. After listening

The burning ship

to hundreds of dharma talks, reading many books, and attending many retreats, the message finally got to me. I realized, at last, that I was on fire with clinging to an old story, with greed for what I thought I deserved, and with hatred of others and myself and the cultural conditioning this came from. My fragile ship, my ego identity, surrounded by the vast and wild sea of desire and entitlement, was aflame with frustration.

I had been identified with the victim/perpetrator duality, spinning round and round on the wheel of *samsara*: of hate, of desperate voracity, of entitlement, resentment, and helplessness. At that energetic level, I saw myself as the victim of the aggressive, perpetrating patriarchy. I was participating in a sadomasochistic dance, resulting in feelings of helplessness, shame, and rage. But I had reached my limit with the frustration of riding this endless wheel, round and round in this repeating pattern of suffering and getting nowhere. I just couldn't do it anymore—not even one more second. Carl Jung said change happens when you actually just can't do it anymore. The fire of frustrated desire had begun to consume my ego.

Jung discovered that the ancient, esoteric, alchemical texts described psychic processes. These texts, he found, traced the stages of spiritual transformation, one of which is called *calcinatio*. This is the stage of fire—the incineration of the old ruling principle in the structure of the psyche, the one to which we cling and with which we identify. That old king ego must die (Edinger, 1985, p. 19). The alchemists described the incineration of our entitlement to power and to gratification of desire. This dovetailed perfectly with Buddhist philosophy.

Once again, I had reached another level of truth. I relinquished the delusional reality of victim/perpetrator in which I was enslaved, where I was prone to emotional victimization by men and internalized androcentrism and, in turn, victimized myself and others with my self-righteousness and blame. The very heat of my frustration consumed itself, much as the flames razed the ship. Now, my default mode, my entitled anger and identity as victim, was gone. I was left without a clue as to who I was or what I wanted. The Zen Buddhists call this "beginner's mind." This was a crisis. I felt fragile and vulnerable. The Buddhist sutra or scripture tells this story: At one time Buddha spoke to a group of a thousand fire worshippers saying, "Monks, everything is ablaze! … Ablaze with what? Ablaze with the fire of passion, the fire of aversion, the fire of delusion" (The Adittapariyaya Sutta , 2000, p. 1143). He advised the fire worshipers to metaphorically tend to their inner rather than outer fires (Adittapariyaya Sutta, 1993).

I moved out of the trance of dissociation. I felt the confusion and paranoia that can result when preconceived patterns of thought and behavior go up in flames. Were my teachers indoctrinating me? From this paranoid place I felt I couldn't ask my analyst or venerable teacher. With my old patterns and reactivity turned to ashes, my default narrative gone, I wasn't sure who to trust, what to expect, and what actions to take. I felt lost.

The alchemists understood this very fragile and vulnerable time could only be survived by connection with a spiritual or transpersonal power. It was the same advice Carl Jung gave to Bill W. and those suffering with alcoholism—to admit one is powerless and to believe that a power greater than oneself could restore sanity. Then, out of the alchemical ash, the stone of creative potential begins to form. The fiery destruction of old patterns, the *prima materia*, has been transformed into the white ash of wisdom and illumination. And over time, in symbolic terms, it becomes a ruby, and then a diamond. The frustrated personality dominated by king ego is consumed. *Calcinatio*, the burning to ash, is a purifying ordeal. By this grace I began to move out of bitterness (Edinger, 1985, pp. 22–45).

I wrote this poem to celebrate my growing capacity to see things as they are:

Civil Disobedience—Satyagraha
Scrambling over boulders in the hot sun to reach you
Sweaty fingers sliding off outcrops,
Old worn boots searching for a foothold
You can't reason someone into loving you.
With my idee fixe and your idee fixe
We're in two bumper cars or we're body slamming into a concrete wall.
Why are there so many obstacles to love?
The wheel of samsara tumbles on.
I want off this merry-go-round of suffering.
Breathing in, I'm here, my boots planted on the mountain.
Breathing out, I'm belayed down the rocky slope.
My body expanding and contracting like the tides, like the universe.
The waves of breath messaging, the salty tears of a woman struggling for freedom
like Gandhi—
on my own salt march to the sea.
I make a bold attempt to end suffering.
Satyagraha, the force born of truth.
In civil disobedience I meditate.
I do no harm
I disobey. I speak truth to power. I AM not passive.

Pegasus flies through the window

Dream: Pegasus Flies Through the Window

After persevering for many years, maybe fifteen or twenty, and working with several Jungian analysts, I dream that the winged horse Pegasus flies through my bedroom window. Pegasus, who was sired by Poseidon. Pegasus, born from Medusa's blood. I'm betting it was from the right vein, which cured, because everywhere this horse struck his foot to the earth a spring of inspiration burst forth—poetry and art and music and dance and spiritual connection. Again, the synchronicity! The horse that had been with me on my raft had transformed into a spiritual force of creativity.

Years into my Buddhist practice and long after finishing my Jungian analytic training, a window had opened, air was flowing, change was happening. My fixed anger and resentment had loosened. I was moving past the claustrophobia of old conditioning.

I must tell you; it was not an easy cult from which to free oneself. I tasted the blood from Medusa's right vein, with its salty power to heal. My heart was opening. I experienced deep compassion for myself and the struggling humans caught in the net of perceptions formed by trauma. I finally understood my spider phobia—I had been like a fly trapped in a spiderweb. The more I struggled, the more entwined I became.

Best yet, I began to experience forgiveness. As Rilke noted, "For these are the moments when something new enters us, something unknown" (Rilke, 2021, p. 65). Something novel and unpredictable was emerging. I was being liberated from the inflated idea that I was innocent, above it all. I was owning my shadow, accepting my limitations, recognizing myself as I am and the world as it is. Problems can't be solved, only outgrown, only seen from a new perspective.

Dream: A Ruby and a New Shakespearean Play

I dream that I find a ruby and a new Shakespearean play. The people in the dream are dressed in Elizabethan garb, and a man offers a woman the gift of a ruby on a sateen pillow—like it was a crown—so valuable.

The alchemical description of the transformation of the personality describes a period of reddening called the *rubedo* (Edinger, 1985, p. 147). It marks the return of the life force, rejuvenation: It happens after we have begun to give up the hopes of the ego's grandiose expectations, realizing they will never be fulfilled and that living is often disappointing and difficult. I was getting past the grief of accepting life as it really is, accepting that I'm an ordinary, flawed human. The salt water of my tears had cleansed and baptized me, a new birth.

Wearing my ruby, I began to love, to connect to a quiet joy, to generosity, kindness, and compassion, especially compassion

A ruby and a new Shakespearean play

for the internalized battles I suffered. I had protectively closed my heart to myself and others. It had been tight and constricted. But now, I found myself being more genuine in my relationships, without effort, without leaning into accommodation or anger. I was reclaiming the jewels that Medusa and I had lost when the feminine was devalued and oppressed by patriarchal power. Spiritual ideas

I'd read on the page became my lived experience—not through willpower, but given to me as a gift. The thought occurred to me, "I guess this is what engaging with the positive masculine feels like." It was like I had a horse to support me.

My culturally conditioned perceptions had produced the way I saw the world. I had not taken the middle road. I had, initially, chosen the path of the feminist interpretation of the Medusa myth and identified as a shamed and angry exile, which thrust me into a rigid, one-sided position. I could still see that level of life—defensive, angry, critical, and wronged—but now desired to get off the eternally spinning wheel of *samsara*. As I sat at a table during a luncheon meeting, friends maligned the speaker and looked to me for validation of their gripes. Although I understood their perceptions because I had so often been there myself, I didn't want to align with that energy. I knew this meant that I would be left out of many conversations and that I might be seen as aloof. A bit of loneliness set in. But my inner critics were quieter. With commitment to the Buddhist path, I could accept my feelings of estrangement and loneliness with compassion, and they were more easily released.

In my mid-seventies, I started to paint these dreams. They came back to me easily. I did it **only** for myself, and it was a soulful and healing process. I found amazing beauty in the little park across the street. I took up the violin, something I had dropped at seven or eight years old when my father sucked the life out of it. I was at peace with him and at peace with myself and the world as it is. I had more energy. And I felt unworldly joy, too, a subtle joy that was not dependent on external conditions. It was about being right with myself, nourishing even in the midst of troubled times—moments of a liberated heart, of space and freedom from striving and pushing away, wonderful ruby moments that have widened to days—but I don't want to misrepresent myself. I'm not an individuated or enlightened being. Not even close!

Gratitude for all my helpers

Dream: Gratitude For All My Helpers and the Swim Team Dream

In my dream I'm in a pool with my swim team. I have been burned so badly that I'm a ball of scars. My teammates take up the task of debridement, cutting away the damaged tissues.

This dream presented how deep my wounding had been, in case I was tempted to deny it or make light of it. I know there is no way I could have done this without this team, the many helpers who have appeared in my life along the way. It has been slow, careful work. Because of all those who have helped me, the hardened scars, the defenses covering shame, fear, and vulnerability have been tended to in both the inner and outer worlds.

I hope you can feel how the archetypes drew me in with their otherworldly energy, yanking me this way and that. Both my Jungian and Buddhist paths helped me to know that the transpersonal isn't separate from the personal. The archetypal patterns can be energizing, but also spellbinding and addictive if not mediated by ethics. I do my best to hold my own and act with compassion rather than reactivity. I still have remnants of my scars, especially the tougher ones. I try to relate to those wounded places with love, kindness, patience, and compassion. Reactivity is transforming through a new and kinder relationship to suffering the normal struggles of life. I heard a Buddhist teacher advise, "Teach with your scars, not with your wounds" (Brensilver, 2024).

I painted the snake necklace to honor the snake goddess and Medusa and to symbolize the beauty and bravery of shedding one's old skin for a new one. And I end my story with my poem of gratitude:

Love Triumphs
Selfishness is leaving through the back door
Love is pushing it out
Compassion is pushing it out
Joy for the happiness of others is pushing it out
Equanimity in the face of longing is pushing it out.
I knew I should get rid of it—
But I couldn't.
"I" wanted—I really wanted
"I" desired

"I" was willful
"I" could have never done it on my own.
I had to be deeply loved and to love.
And suffer disappointment for the good of all beings.
Love trumped the "I"
What the Fuck says "I"
Watch out what you ask for.

Liberated by Love

Jacqueline Wright

My external world looks picture perfect. I'm standing in the middle passage of my life, a married woman with three "almost" grown children, a Doctorate in Higher Education and Counseling, and an interesting and challenging job involved in innovative work in the higher education department of the university. As wife, mother, daughter, and educator, my life is rich and challenging, and the joys and challenges of balancing the different roles brings a sense of fulfillment.

But if we bravely and carefully peel back the curtain on this well-constructed persona, it doesn't look so perfect. Underneath, I'm a mess. I live in an interior world filled with deep sadness, anger, and confusion. My heart aches. I feel alone. Nights are filled with dreams of not being able to move, of being enclosed in narrow hallways, stuck in old-fashioned school desks or in elevator shafts, unable to move up or down or to make something happen. Tears flow unexpectedly—in the bathroom, in public spaces, in conversations with friends and family. This isn't the person I've always known myself to be— one who has generally moved through daily crisis and life's passages with calmness and equanimity—but not now.

Why do I feel so sad and immobilized? I recognize that there are cracks in my marriage that have been in the making for some time. A few years ago, my husband was offered a new job that required traveling all week and a relocation of the family to a new location every two years. He seemed quite excited about it, but I felt an immediate resistance and feared what the proposed disruptive arrangements might mean for me, our marriage, and our family. My sense of security in the relationship felt threatened, and I felt betrayed in some way. Wasn't marriage supposed to be a reciprocal relationship? I struggled to find my place in this proposed arrangement. Do I support my husband's promotion and the conditions that it imposes on me and the family, or do I fight against it? Do I leave the marriage? Confrontation wasn't something I was used to, and it felt scary. I felt very alone in trying to make a decision that I knew would change my life pretty drastically. But in the end, after a good bit of agonizing, I decided that the responsible thing to do was to support my husband and keep the family together. I silenced the inner voices that said, "no," put on the uniform of the good wife, and did my best to make it work.

When it came time for the family to make a fourth move to another state, the resistance and feelings of anger and resentment that I had been pushing aside came bursting forth with a fury. I was so tired of not having control over my life, and I was also exhausted with the constant changes. Our family life was suffering, and so was the marital relationship. Since my husband was only home on weekends, most of the work to get settled into the new locations had fallen on me. Finally, I could no longer contain the feelings welling up in me, and I remember standing in the shower one day, letting the hot water run over my body and saying out loud, "I will not live this way any longer!" This time I said, "No, I'm not moving," which meant that I stayed in our present home with the children, and my husband moved to another location. We continued with our commuter marriage and spent weekends and holidays together.

Almost immediately after I made this decision, I enrolled in school to get my master's degree the age of thirty-nine. This required more of my time and attention and began to conflict with my ability and desire to play the role of corporate wife and attend meetings and events with my husband. Consequently, my husband felt betrayed and resentful, straining the relationship even more.

I also started Jungian analysis, which began the journey of illuminating my hidden subjective world. As my story unfolded in the safety of the analytic container, I gradually realized how I had learned to suppress my own desires and emotions because they felt too dangerous. As I brought more of my feelings of sadness, anger, and frustration into the room, I became aware of how those hidden and threatening emotions, if expressed, could inform me and help me make decisions. Then a dream occurred that upended my life and changed its trajectory:

> *I'm standing on a wooden deck that runs along the outside of a rather small or medium-sized boat. I look up to see water flowing rapidly down a man-made flume on the side of a hill that is very close to the boat. The water is flowing with a lot of force, and I'm enjoying the movement of the water and the feeling of wetness against my face from the water.*
>
> *All at once I realize that the water is overflowing the flume and coming into the boat. It begins to fill the area that I'm standing in, and it is rising around me at a rapid pace. I'm alarmed and then start to feel a sense of panic that the boat will eventually fill up with water and sink. I quickly decide that the only way to*

> *save myself is to go below and tie myself down with a man's belt.*
> *Then I find myself standing in the lower part of the boat beside a horizontal iron bar that is about waist high, with a man's belt encircling the bar and my right arm. I stand there like a good soldier, confident that I'm safe, watching the water as it begins rising around me. I'm breathing rapidly when the water reaches my face. When it is right under my nose I suddenly realize that if I stay in this position I will most certainly drown!*
> *I wake in a state of terror.*

After a few minutes, I catch my breath and calm down a bit. Then I get back into the dream experience and *dream it forward* as I've learned to do.

I unbuckle the belt and then find myself standing barefoot on a wooden gangplank that leads away from the boat. As I walk to the end of the gangplank, I look up and see before me a vast stretch of barren land. The ground seems packed down and extends endlessly before me. Something inside me releases as I look into that vast, empty space. The openness and the nothingness that lies before me feels like a new universe, one that is unending and undemanding, like a place waiting for a new story to be written, a blank canvas waiting to be painted, or a barren land waiting to be dug up and planted. I feel the solid wooden boards of the gangplank underneath my feet. My entire body tingles with excitement as I take in the image and the possibilities that stretch out before me. I take a long, deep breath that comes freely and easily now. The image, even with its very earthy, sensory elements, feels numinous, an archetypal space unbounded by ordinary limits and time. I feel at home here, at home with myself.

Later, as I consciously begin to take in the dream, I have an immediate association to an actual site that I have observed many times driving along a highway in east Tennessee. It is a unique structure, a man-made system that consists of a sort of shelf or flume that has been carved into the side of the mountain and stretches twelve miles along a narrow river gorge. Its purpose is to capture river water from the Ocoee River, a fast-flowing stream that originates deep in Georgia, and force it through the narrow flume to a hydro plant in Tennessee in order to create electricity for the surrounding area.

I quickly make the association of this man-made construction to my own internal system that is failing to contain the powerful, excruciating, debilitating, overwhelming energies and emotions that I have desperately been trying to contain. Remembering the power of the flowing water evokes that sense of relief that I have been wishing for, even though it carries the prospect of drowning. I also recognize that my attempts to control the life energy that was pushing its way into my consciousness is what has rendered me powerless to move forward in my life. The dream has shaken me, but I feel grateful for the relief.

But the most disturbing element of the dream is that the immediate solution I think of to save myself from drowning, which is to "go below" and tie myself down with a man's belt. I can now feel my resistance to this idea that wasn't present in the dream itself. First of all, it suggests a quick surrender and perhaps a habitual solution to feeling threatened or overwhelmed, which is to find a quick answer and shut down the emotion. A man's belt suggests a man's world and communicates qualities of control, authority, and power. I had been living my life in a man's world, silencing my own voice, suppressing my own aspirations and desires, believing that my compliance would save me. My response in the dream also illuminates the fact that I didn't yet have the tools I needed to confront the shadow of that masculine world. The iron post seemed to be part of the construction of the boat and what was "holding everything together." I wonder, is it pointing to the steely hold my internal construction has on me? For example, was it my immersion in higher education, that focused world of the intellect, that was represented by being stuck in school desks? Or was it my belief that "dad" was always going to be there when I needed something? In the dream, I stand like a good soldier, waiting with confidence that these masculine elements will save me from drowning. How did I arrive at this point, and who is this good soldier who stands mutely and patiently waiting for her demise?

My first thoughts about the symbolism of that dream went to the patriarchal society that has shaped me. I learned early on that my value and safety depended upon following the roles and rules set out for me, which included deferring to males and giving priority to being a wife and mother. My mother was my first instructor, and society's rules about women's roles and ways of behaving were pretty rigidly enforced by her. Her attitude was clearly visible when she tried to convince my father that sending me to college would be a waste of money because I would only get married. In her mind, secretarial school was a better option. In retrospect, I can now see how her own life force was kept in check by the roles she tried to fulfill and how it fueled the envy I felt from her later in life as I broke some of those tradition-bound rules.

Thankfully, I was saved by my father, who quietly supported my path. He was a very quiet man who spoke softly and rarely expressed his own ideas, and certainly not any emotions! This was the way I had responded in my dream. I clearly modeled myself after him and he was always there for me and eager to help in any way he could. However, the dream's message was that emulating his repression of voice and emotion had not served me. My mother, in contrast, was funny, vivacious, and had a playful nature that I enjoyed, but her occasional and unpredictable outbursts of anger frightened me. The outbursts were not terribly aggressive, but they seemed to come out of nowhere and felt "out of control" in comparison to my father's reasoned reactions. I quickly formed an inner rule not to be like her! That meant keeping a tight lid on my own emotional responses.

So, I could easily relate the controlled water system portrayed in my dream to my early family life. With the exception of my mother's occasional outbursts, emotions were rarely expressed. Family discussions were practically nonexistent. There were implicit guidelines, but no stated rules for me to follow. I was more or less on my own in terms of making decisions about my life, and I parented myself with some pretty stringent rules. I was aware that my internal system of control as depicted in the dream took over my personality and life quite early. More importantly, the dream pointed to the dangers that ensue from trying to live such a controlled life.

My work with the dream led me to June Singer and her book, *Modern Woman in Search of a Soul*, in which she described what it was like to live astride two worlds: the visible, known, ego-driven world with its drives, ambitions, and goals, and the invisible world of the unconscious that contained longings, possibilities, and images. This is where I found myself, living astride these two worlds, searching for soul, longing for that unknowable world of mystery that I dreamed of as a child and that I was drawn to from an early age. It was the mystical world where anything was possible, where there were no rules or correct ways of doing things, and where anything could be experienced as real and true. It was the secret world of imagination that came to life in me: looking out of my bedroom window at the stars, pondering those larger questions about who or what ruled that large expanse of night sky, relishing in the expansiveness of that unknown world. It was also the secret world that was ignited by the *Grimm's Fairy Tales* book (Grimm & Grimm, 1812/1944), a treasured gift that I received and devoured in my very early years. This subjective, intuitive world that I lived in seemed to have no place or resonance in my predominately sensate family. But the colorful and imaginative images that I held inside helped me live more easily in a family so different from me. Sharing my inner world also collided with my need for approval, so to avoid possible embarrassment or conflict, I repressed the very parts of myself that would have brought a feeling of joy about living in accordance with my natural gifts. I also repeated this pattern in my marriage, where I'd often replaced playfulness and imagination with work and responsibility, resulting in a feeling of loneliness.

My dream had sent a clear message that this unlived side of my personality that had been carefully channeled and controlled was now threatening to overwhelm me if I didn't live it out consciously. It also conveyed the message that I had to be my own rescuer, let go of those traditional roles defined by a male-dominated society and define myself in terms of my own interests, talents, and capacities. I knew intuitively after the dream that my inner work was to explore and till that undeveloped earth depicted in the last part of my dream. That image had allowed me to see my world from a totally different perspective, one that was not restrictive but inviting, filled with endless possibilities. So, I unbuckled the metaphorical belt and opened the door to the unknown and a journey of self-discovery. As Mary Oliver (2020, p. 349) wrote about in her beautiful poem "The Journey," I did the only thing I could do, which was to follow my own inner voice and save myself.

Soon after the dream occurred, I'm riding in the car with my husband. I heard myself saying, "You know what I'd like to do? I'd like to go to Zürich to pursue analytic training!" My question seemed to come out of nowhere and surprised me almost as much as it did him. I felt charged with some unfamiliar energy. Even more surprising was his response. "Well, why don't you go?" It felt like a memorable moment—when my soul declared itself and spoke out—and when my husband responded with support, it felt as though the universe was saying, "Yes!"

That moment launched me into action, and I started making preparations to go to Zürich. I actually knew very little about the training program, and my intention was to enroll as an auditor to see if it was something I wanted to explore further. Little did I or my husband know that I would leave him and our three children, who were on the verge of launching themselves in the world, and spend the next five and a half years there. My decision was a sharp turn from being the responsible wife and mother, and I realized that it could be judged negatively, but I had repressed my emotions for too long and now had to nurture what was becoming alive in me. I carried Rūmī's words in a pocket of my mind as I moved forward:

> Let yourself be silently drawn
> by the stronger pull of what you really love. (Rūmī, 1995, p. 51)

I entered my new world in Zürich with enthusiasm and excitement. One of my most vivid memories is the experience of walking into my very own apartment. I opened the door and just stood in the entrance for a long time, trying to take in the fact that for the first time in my life I now had a space that was all mine! Wow! I breathed in the fact that my life would be determined by no one other than myself, and I could design it any way I wished.

The sense of liberation, freedom, and control over my new world was exhilarating. I listened and tended to my own needs; I rediscovered my love of nature on my long walks through the woods; I relished the silence and embraced my introverted self. As Mary Oliver said in her poem, "there was a new voice" which I slowly recognized as my own (Oliver, 2020, p. 349). Like a worn and tattered dress that no longer fits or hold its shape, the old identity, with its old scripts about how I was supposed to live my life, slowly began to unravel. This separateness was what I needed to gain access to my own soul.

I'm now a long way from that part of my personal story, yet I'm more aware than ever that the myth that has given credence to the struggles and joyous moments in my life is the Eros and Psyche myth, a well-known story with varied interpretations. It has been helpful in illuminating the patterns and archetypal energies that have driven and moved me. I view the myth as a metaphor about the journey and transformation of a seeker for soul. It reveals the role of love in our lives.

The story begins with a young princess, Psyche, in despair.[3] *No one has asked for Psyche's hand in marriage, and she has angered Aphrodite, the mother of Eros and the goddess of beauty, love, and fertility. Her father seeks an answer from the oracle, who decrees that Psyche is to be married to a monster. She goes to meet her death and instead is carried away by Eros, who opens her up to a world of possibilities and pleasure. But their relationship only takes place in the dark, and Psyche has been warned to never see Eros in the light of day. One day she is visited by her envious sisters, who persuade her that she is really married to a monster and must kill him. Psyche is swayed by their arguments and approaches Eros one night with a knife and oil lamp. When she shines the light on him, she recognizes him as a god and falls in love with him. But a scalding drop of oil from the lamp awakens him, and when he sees what Psyche has done, he vanishes. Psyche mourns his loss and sets out on a journey to find him.*

Psyche is initially depicted as a young woman who accepts her fate passively, without any protest or defiance. This lack of reaction is echoed in my personal story of how passively I accepted

[3] The name "Psyche" here also represents the human psyche.

the roles that I felt had been assigned me. A vivid example is how I stepped out of college after three years and into marriage without any doubts or questions. That lack of agency continued into the early years of marriage, until I finally found my voice in the shower and stood up for my own needs.

Psyche's relationship to Eros initially takes place in darkness, which represents a state of blissful unconsciousness. This blissful state is interrupted by a visit from Psyche's sisters, who are described as being unhappy with their lives. They would gladly leave the husbands they are married to. Neumann suggests that these wicked figures "represent a violated matriarchal psyche living in service to the patriarchy" (Neumann, 1952/1956, p. 71). Their angry, vindictive advice to Psyche about how to kill Eros stands in contrast to her unquestioning trust and passivity. We can easily see them as Psyche's shadow and can imagine the internal conflict that it creates in her. Eros has already implored her not to listen to what the sisters say, which indicates Psyche's resistance to consciousness of the situation and a desire to maintain the status quo. But it is the energy of the angry sisters that wakes Psyche up and initiates the action to break the taboo and shine the light on Eros, freeing herself from her unconscious state. This suggests a moment of psychic transformation and "the beginning of a higher feminine consciousness" (Neumann, 1952/1956, p. 74). Psyche's actions also create a separation between her and Eros, sending them on separate journeys to heal their own wounds. It is their related wounds that have brought them together, and it is this unconscious bond that must be dissolved.

I am thankful for my own angry sisters who finally showed up and expressed their voices. I heard them in my dreams saying, "Why are you so confused? You're stuck in old patterns. You're not going anywhere. You need to wake up and figure out why you're feeling so stuck. Take some action!" I also experienced that moment in my marriage when I made the decision not to move households and to pursue my own interests and desires as the beginning of the development of my own higher feminine consciousness. I had silenced my own voice in order to avoid conflict and heartbreak, and that had played a big part in the unconscious marriage we were living in. I finally found the courage to turn the light on our situation, which created a separation and provided the space that we both needed to break those unconscious ways of functioning.

When Psyche begins her journey to find Eros, she's bereft and suicidal. After the river frustrates her attempt at suicide, she meets Pan, the nature god, the lover of life, earth, and living creatures. He suggests that she submit to Eros and advises her to continue to seek him and win his love.

I can connect this part of the myth to that moment in the car with my husband, when I unexpectedly declared my desire to pursue Jungian training. Pan's question, "Why don't you submit to Eros?" had finally reached my consciousness, and my desire had decisively found its voice. My husband's reply, "Well, why don't you go?" echoes and supports Pan's advice to continue to seek what you love. This exchange released something in me. My tendency to see my husband as a captor or an obstacle to my development dissolved. I was no longer a victim, and he was now a consciously supportive presence that changed my image of love. I could now relinquish that unconscious identity and fusion, make my wishes known, and move toward my own journey and individual tasks.

After Psyche leaves Pan, she meets Aphrodite's handmaids, who turn her over to Aphrodite. Aphrodite then assigns her tasks to complete. The first task requires sorting a pile of seeds, a daunting task that requires selecting, evaluating, and creating order. But Psyche receives help from ants, which are symbols of the instinctual world, indicating that Psyche's task requires a different kind of consciousness, not the same kind of mental ordering I had been using.

Like Psyche, I was in foreign territory, and I had to feel my way forward. I was faced with a muddle of questions about myself that needed sorting: Who am I really? What are my desires? What are the qualities that tend to hold me back from achieving my desires? What are these opposing energies in me? Sorting questions like these was a slow process and required trusting my feelings and intuitions without over-analyzing or second-guessing them. Then it meant making decisions that were in harmony with myself and my own desires and needs.

Psyche's second task is to gather wisps of wool from the rams, which symbolize a potentially destructive power of the masculine. This time she is helped by the reed, which is connected to water and is a feminine symbol. The reed advises Psyche not to confront the rams directly, but to wait until the sun goes down and then gather the fleece that had been caught on the twigs of tree branches where the rams had sought shade.

Understanding that I needed to claim some of that aggressive masculine power has been an important task for me. Living alone for a time allowed me the space that I needed to confront and understand my fears of "being out of control" and helped me gain a clearer picture of this complex. Once I got over some of my fear of anger, I was able to appreciate it and express it more confidently. That helped diminish my fear of someone else's anger and ability to either confront it or find creative ways to use it or avoid it. But I have also learned that sometimes I embody my mother and express my own "out of control" anger toward others. Now I can usually laugh about it.

Psyche's third task requires her to fill a crystal vase with water from the source of rivers in the underworld. The water flows from the highest crag of a huge mountain that is guarded by watchful snakes (or dragons). Psyche is paralyzed by the impossibility of the task but is aided by an eagle, which is associated with a masculine energy and spirit. It is the eagle that soars past the watchful snakes to the top of the mountain and returns with the urn filled with water.

This task mirrors the emotional turmoil I faced in my dream when the rushing waters confronted me with the possibility of death. The rush of water that Psyche faces is described in the myth as coming from "a rock of measureless height, rough, slippery, and inaccessible"; it "vomited forth a hideous stream that ... had worn out a narrow channel for its path and, thus concealed, rushed secretly into the neighboring valley" (Neumann, 1952/1956, p. 45). The waters had voices that cried out and forbade approach, "'Beware!' and 'Fly!' and lastly 'Thou art doomed to die!'" (Neumann, 1952/1956, p. 45). This description is stunningly similar to the constructed water channel in my dream and also carries the same threat of death.

The water that Psyche is required to capture represents a stream of vital energy that is described by Neumann as that "uncontainable energy of the unconscious, the life stream [that] possesses a specific symbolism in relation to Psyche" (Neumann, 1952/1956, p. 103–104). Psyche "as feminine vessel, is ... to give form and rest to what is formless and flowing ... to give form to life" (Neumann, 1952/1956, p. 103).

The tasks Psyche faced resonate deeply with my own experiences, and the interplay of the energies depicted in the myth have mirrored my own internal struggle to "give form to life." My own journey has been about recognizing the necessity of balancing both feminine and masculine energies in myself. Integrating these energies requires not only understanding what they offer but the need to learn how to use them to achieve a more integrated self.

In this task it is the eagle that faces the snakes (or dragons), soars to the top of the mountain, and returns with the urn filled with water. This image of masculine energy suggests strength, assertiveness, and the ability to confront and navigate challenges.

By harnessing masculine energy, I was able to untie the metaphorical belt binding me and appreciate the life force that is depicted within that flow of unleashed emotions in my dream.

Psyche's fourth task is to make the perilous trip to the Underworld and bring back something that has been hidden in the depth of Hades—Persephone's beauty box. Persephone is the queen of the underworld and represents Aphrodite's shadow. The tower advises Psyche what to take and what she must do on this journey. In this instance Psyche must help herself and not respond to the needs of others, but rather be conscious of her own goals and stay on her own path. She manages to retrieve the beauty box and leave the Underworld; however, Psyche disobeys Aphrodite's rule, opens the box, and falls into a deep sleep.

The beauty of Psyche at the beginning of the myth was a superficial beauty, without depth or insight, a beauty determined and valued by the patriarchal world Psyche lived in. This angered the goddess Aphrodite, the goddess of love and beauty. Persephone was also known for her beauty, which was a key element in the myth of her abduction by Hades. Her residence in the Underworld suggests that she now has a depth of beauty that embraces her whole nature—her innocence, vulnerability, strengths, and weaknesses. Psyche's trip to the Underworld represents a completion of the tasks that will liberate her from living in an illusory world of admiration and self-doubt. Her decision to again break a taboo and open Persephone's beauty box suggests to me that she is ready to claim her own darkness, her whole self.

What did I find in my own beauty box when I dared to open it? I found a love of self that had been hidden beneath layers of self-doubt and societal expectations. I found a new appreciation for my initial innocence and vulnerability, recognizing them not as weaknesses but as essential parts of my identity. I found a new relationship with my "dark sister," the shadowy aspects of myself that I had disowned. I found an appreciation for the trials and challenges that forced me to find the inner strength and resourcefulness I needed for another level of aliveness.

Eros goes to Psyche, awakens her, and urges her to complete her last task of delivering Persephone's beauty box to Aphrodite. Meanwhile, Eros returns to Olympus to seek Zeus's approval of the union. Zeus gives his blessing and sends Hermes to bring Psyche to heaven. Their marriage is celebrated, and soon a daughter is born to them. She is called Pleasure, symbolizing the union of love and the fulfillment of Psyche's journey towards wholeness and true connection.

When I returned from Zürich, I had to weave together what felt like the old me and the new me, which required finding my place in my family, establishing myself as an analyst, and making space for my relational life. But this time I wasn't carrying a suitcase full of angry feelings and resentment. Instead, I was bringing the new and developing child within, the one that now carried the joy of discovery, play, and imagination. There was new energy for relationships and new experiences. But I still felt the need for solitude and my own physical space to consolidate the changes that had occurred in me. So, I made a decision to settle down in a different town than where my husband lived. This was not a new arrangement for us, since we had maintained separate households previously. I could now appreciate how our separate living arrangements had actually allowed the necessary space we needed to break out of our unconscious marriage. We now recognized and accepted each other's differences and needs, but our care for each other and for the family remained intact.

The support that my husband offered when I expressed my desire to pursue training never wavered. He was the glue that held the family together while I was away, fulfilling parental duties and extended family responsibilities. Upon my return he helped me settle into a new city, and I did the same for him in a different city. We maintained our close connection, and family gatherings and celebrations continued to occur in both locations. We did finalize a divorce a few years after my return, but the story of our relationship didn't end there. The vibration of love for each other echoed through our lives, with daily check-in phone calls, until my husband's death a few years ago. We didn't follow the traditional script for a couple. Instead, we each followed our individual paths, yet maintained the strong bonds that had brought us together in the beginning.

The myth of Eros and Psyche suggests that love creates a perpetual process of development and evolution and goes through many stages. The ruptures that occur in Psyche's story also point to the necessary separations we may need to go through in order to grow into our ability for true connection and to realize our full potential. A true marriage evolves out of elements that have been separated and made their own individual journeys. Rilke also captures this beautifully:

> *For one human being to love another: that is perhaps the most difficult of all our tasks, the ultimate, the last test and proof, the work for which all other work is but preparation. For this reason young people who are beginners in everything cannot know love: they have to learn it ... but learning time is always a long, secluded time, and so loving for a long while ahead and far on into life is—solitude, intensified and deepened loneness for him who loves. Love is at first not anything that means merging, giving over, and uniting with another (for what would a union be of something unclarified and unfinished, still subordinate?). (Rilke, 1934/1954, pp. 53–54)*

I feel immense gratitude for the love that has supported and guided me through my journey of self-discovery and self-compassion. I am grateful for my husband's willingness to stand in the unknown with me. The maturing of our relationship occurred through the challenges we faced to recognize our individual wounds, defenses, and complexes. We bonded through respect for our individual journeys. The separations allowed and created reunion that was liberating for us both.

Concluding Remarks in Her Honor

Marilyn Marshall

None of the storytellers could have imagined the distinctively personal experiences that would awaken each of us to ourselves and to a consciousness of a divine *Feminine* dwelling within. With intimations of *her* in childhood and invitations throughout our lives to relate to her mysteries, the archetypal feminine calls us again and again into the fullness of our nature. She has been eternally there in our grandmothers' trials, in our mothers' struggles, and in the roles generations of women have embraced, questioned, or rejected. Hidden in the myths and the fairy tales of old, the heavenly pantheons and the underworld chambers, the darkness and light of the archetypal feminine has permeated life and has lived, too, in the unconscious shadows: La Sirène lights candles in the sea, quelling the thunderous storm; Persephone, queen of the underworld, attends at a daughter's descent; the sacred prostitutes of the goddesses of love sanctify sex and love; a mother's prayer to Sophia blesses her daughter's birth and desire; the single-breasted stranger evokes the body and the tears for the lost feminine; Demeter Erinys demands more of love; Medusa's blood destroys and heals; and Aphrodite sets the arduous tasks for reunion with Eros.

The effects of collective consciousness, religious beliefs, and parental patterns of relating are prominent aspects of our stories. There is no avoidance of this reality for any of us, and we have lived the first half of our lives in degrees of acceptance or rejection, responding to its ideals for the normal, the acceptable, the agreeable, and the expected role of a girl and a woman in a man's world. Our mothers and fathers are the first source of these legacies and expectations, both affecting the girl's psychological development and, later, challenging the woman's consciousness. In that particular stage of life we have lived, for the most part, unconsciously—acquiring an ego identity and persona that establishes a sense of self and seeking love and/or power that provides a sense of fulfillment. In this endeavor we repress many of the negative and positive aspects of the feminine deemed bad, inferior, weak, unacceptable. We close the door on them, and yet they slip into our dreams and relationships as unconscious shadow selves that we avoid or deny. This works for a time—until it doesn't: until the moral dilemma, the sudden illness, the amazing dream; until the stagnation, the empty nest, the heartbreaking loss, or the final and consequential "no more."

We have lived many decades since then with gratitude for our evolving consciousness of the particular voices, images, and manifestations of the archetypal feminine. This book is a response to a summons from *her* to engage in the difficult tasks of expressing a part of her-story and to re-member these pivotal experiences of discovery and embodiment for further synthesis. In a zeitgeist of patriarchal attitudes in which her divine images and principles continue to be devalued, categorized, and pathologized, our desire to personally claim her significance and authority has encouraged us to write a part of our stories—in honor of *her*. These experiences have been a gift of and a tribute to the complexities of love.

Part of this complexity is love's expression in the invitations, initiations, and transformations of instinctual, sexual experience. We come to know our bodies and ourselves in unique ways through its sparks and flames. As Jungians, we tend to focus on the spiritual aspects of sex—and that is invaluable. However, to avoid or dismiss the instinctual life of sex maintains the split between body and spirit. Our stories consciously bring forth the passion, desire, and the pleasure of the erotic psyche that has been repressed by collective and religious attitudes that continue to place sex in the rigid category of sin—unless experienced in marriage and unless with a partner of the opposite sex. We all have a sexual complex, having inherited and experienced conscious and unconscious attitudes about sexuality that have affected our relationship to the erotic and to ourselves. And these attitudes have influenced our capacity to claim our own experience and speak about it—until recently. Women's instinctual desires and emotional constellations in sex, consequences of its natural and its shadow aspects and the encounters with and effects of its abuse, magnify its complexity and demand our conscious reflections and responses. Thus, the sexual topics and material offered herein are part of our desire to lay shameless claim to this aspect of the repressed feminine.

From its instinctual, bodily experience to its emotional landscape to its spiritual meaning, sex is honored by the sacred prostitutes of the goddesses of love as an expression of that divine love. As a powerful force in life in its ability to create pleasure in different realms of the psyche, sexual energy is a dynamic catalyst for the movement of psychic energy.

Jung remarks, "there is a close association between sexual instinct and the striving for wholeness. With the exception of religious longings, nothing challenges modern man more consciously and personally than sex" (Jung, 1958/1970, para. 653). This association to wholeness is a two-edged sword for women. As we've shared through our stories, a woman's sexual experiences outside of marriage are most often criticized and judged by patriarchal attitudes and stamped by projections and shame, distorting her connection to wholeness. And her spiritual longing is compromised by the religious structures, belief systems, and rules created by men and personified by their perspectives of divinity.

Whereas Jung found hope in the Catholic Church's doctrine of the Assumption of Mary, elevating the feminine to join the trinitarian masculine of the Christian tradition, only the *sublime* image of the Virgin Mary represents the divine feminine in that heavenly pantheon; the earthy, instinctual aspects of the feminine, some of which are illuminated in these pages, are relegated to the shadow, split off from the fullness of *her* nature. These characteristics beckon a woman's desire for a deeper connection to herself through a relatedness to and assimilation of those unconscious aspects.

Unmistakably notable in our pivotal experiences of feminine consciousness and the complexities of love are the influences and tensions provided by the images and principles of the divine masculine: Yahweh, God the Father, Allah, Zeus, Hades, and Poseidon, as well as those of Jesus, Muhammad, and the Buddha. The psychic reality of the inner masculine is certainly an integral part of a woman's wholeness and offers her an awareness of a very different perspective and challenge. Flesh and blood male figures in our lives capture our projections of this *other*, of the archetypes' positive and negative characteristics: the compassionate father of Christian love, the caring young Muslim in a foreign land, the Jesuit priest's tarot image, the Buddhist teacher's wisdom, the supportive husband at a time of decision—and, the thunderous father of Jewish trauma, the serial predator of Hades's darkness, the lover's "ghosting" of the heart's longing—as well as the unquestionable power of the Church fathers and the ambitious power of the governing sons of Zeus.

However, the inner psychic representations of these archetypal influences prove most crucial for consciousness as a woman learns to confront and relate to the animus in its many destructive and creative attributes revealed in her thoughts and in her dreams: the X-Acto Man, the sado-masochistic ruler on his throne of control, and the soldier, soldiering on—as well as a message from Hemingway, the meeting with the Inner Secret

Lover, the bull's gore of revelation, and the winged horse, Pegasus. The relationship to these masculine aspects can only be realized through an awareness of their presence and a curiosity about those thoughts, ideas, or dreams that assault or support a woman's sense of self—all the while holding one's feminine consciousness.

One of the richest sources of consciousness permeating our stories is the value of feelings. Our awareness and experience of emotions and the bodily sensations they inhabit reveal their relationships to the deeper resources of the unconscious. Each of us has struggled with their significance and their message to face the characteristics of the archetypal feminine and masculine. These feelings engage us in the *experience* of life rather than, simply, the knowledge of it happening to and around us, and their fires can initiate and inform the processes of transformation and healing. However, access to this emotional life can be difficult due to its repression by psychic defenses formed in response to early childhood trauma. These defenses have served as protection against the full force and emotional impact of the traumatic experience that the vulnerable child cannot withstand. Figures and motifs in our dreams, as well as the encounters with our complexes, illustrate emotional outbreaks and defensive protection from the wounds of love and, as we've described, offer us opportunities for the conscious experience of those emotions. Much like the aid that Psyche received during her torments with each impossible task from Aphrodite, we have faith that, in time, help and support will come from the unconscious that will transcend the painful tensions of the labors of love and reunite us with Eros.

The implications of these stories for modern women are significant in their unique accounts of both the feminine and masculine archetypal realities that intimately affect one's life. We are born into a particular collective consciousness created by the evolving relationships between these psychic energies, and the narratives shared in these pages describe the indelible significance of and struggles in a woman's conscious development of her feminine identity. The dynamics within and between these archetypal principles and the tensions they provide in relationship to oneself and to others invite a woman to take seriously her inner world and its psychic processes of transformation. These influences, via numinous experiences, dreams, and the complexes informed by their characteristics, are, metaphorically, clothed differently throughout generations; however, the archetypes enact their eternal dramas in modern life, and our consideration of their stories through Jung's method of amplification enriches our own with new and insightful possibility and meaning.

These different stories are part of each woman's inviolate mysteries, pivotal accounts of our struggles to honor the divine feminine and to embrace the complexities of love. This path has been a challenge, as our secrets have exposed, and our desire for wholeness, for relatedness to the unconscious, continues. When we'd agreed together to write this personal volume, which to us felt needed in the collective at this time, we were unaware of the courage necessary to give voice to the intimate story that wanted to be told for the Jungian community or any others interested in the emerging experiences and expressions of the feminine. Nevertheless, our efforts in this work have continued to reveal ourselves to us, deepening our process of individuation—relating to *her*, to *him*, and to love:

> *She had no right breast, only something that looked like a reconstructed nipple on her chest, and her left breast drooped well below her waist. Tears streamed down my face as I drove away. I longed to talk to her: I imagined that she could tell me secret things. She seemed to carry herself with such dignity! This woman stirred something deep within me. It was the world of the feminine that I met as the stranger: Hers*

is the world of emotions and feelings, of valuation, of the instincts and the body. This world involves connectedness and a relatedness to and empathy for ourselves and others. I had become a true obedient daughter of the world of logos, of patriarchal ideas, principles, and laws that had obscured and truncated my feminine self. – Janice

I opened my mouth to say I wasn't prepared to state a symbol, but instead I said very clearly, "I choose the symbol of the sacred prostitute." I could hardly believe it! Those were my words, but who had said them? I was so stunned that I barely remembered the discussion afterward. It was as if an inner voice had chosen my symbol for me. However, I was quite unaware of that repressed image, her energy and dynamics and the real personification of the feminine within me. The sacred prostitute was the personification and advocate of the goddess of love. – Nancy

I return . . . to the abiding love that withstands the errors, the wrong turns, the misguided choices, and the moments of shadow possession so severe that one does not, at times, remember who one is. I have, over the course of my life, found my way to my own voice, well aware of the refrains of my father's and mother's voices within my own. Finding one's voice does, I believe, walk hand in hand with finding one's authority. But in what does one's own authority lie? Experience perhaps, a willingness to question, to face uncertainties, to not believe the lie of desolation, that one is alone. – Carolyn

My experience of the Whinnying Woman and the mandala identified her unmistakable place in the center of my wholeness, my Self, and her message of my strangled love gave me more of that wholeness. She came at a time when I would learn the significance and challenge of that message in relation, especially, to the animus. And I am grateful, so grateful. – Marilyn

During this extensive time of process and insight I found my true love. He introduced himself to me in a dream during a five-minute nap on an airline flight. I happened to be struggling with yet another love affair just having gone down in flames. He said his name exactly like this: "I am THE INNER SECRET LOVER OR THE SECRET INNER LOVER." – Susan

After persevering for many years, maybe fifteen or twenty, and working with several Jungian analysts, I dream that the winged horse Pegasus flies through my bedroom window. Pegasus, who was sired by Poseidon. Pegasus, born from Medusa's blood. I'm betting it was from the right vein, which cured ... – Barbara

What did I find in my own beauty box when I dared to open it? I found a love of self that had been hidden beneath layers of self-doubt and societal expectations. I found a new appreciation for my initial innocence and vulnerability, recognizing them not as weaknesses but as essential parts of my identity. I found a new relationship with my "dark sister," the shadowy aspects of myself that I had disowned. I found an appreciation for the trials and challenges that forced me to find the inner strength and resourcefulness I needed for another level of aliveness. – Jacqueline

> *I can say to you that it was La Sirène calling me from my bed, her candles burning in the sea. Her way reminds my body of its ability to re-member, over and over, the gift of being heard, the miracle of being found. And that this is the work, our individual, ongoing struggle to keep psyche's sacred call and response alive in each of us. – Constance*

As Jungian analysts, we are aware, of course, that projections of shadow and negative animus are probable and that various other interpretations of our dreams, imaginings, and complexes are plausible. However, we stand individually and together as women on a journey with *her*, and we claim her integrity, authority, and our unfolding feminine consciousness of *her* character offered to us for wholeness. We also stand as analysts formed by the experiences of our lives and transformed by the depths of psyche through Jungian analysis, and we speak of and for the individual suffering of the work and the pleasure of its many riches.

A Summary of the Eros and Psyche Myth

Marilyn Marshall

The myth of Eros and Psyche was first depicted in Greek art in the 4th century BCE, but the most well-known version of the story was written in the 2nd century AD by the Roman author Lucius Apuleius in his book, Metamorphoses, better known by its title, The Golden Ass. I have used Greek names for the characters instead of the Roman names used by Apuleius.

In a certain city lived a king and queen who had three daughters. The youngest was named Psyche. She was so beautiful that people worshipped her as if she were Aphrodite. Because of this, Aphrodite's altars were neglected and lay bare. This angered Aphrodite, and she summoned her son Eros and told him to have Psyche consumed with passion for the vilest of men.

Psyche was unhappy, because no king or prince or lover came forward to claim her for marriage. Her two older sisters had been betrothed to kings and gotten married. Psyche was lonely, and grew to loathe her loveliness. So her father, who was worried that perhaps the heavens were angry, sought the god of the Delphic Oracle to send a husband to wed his daughter.

> The god, Apollo, responded thus:
> *On some high crag, O king, set forth the maid,*
> *In all the pomp of funeral robes arrayed.*
> *Hope for no bridegroom born of mortal seed,*
> *But fierce and wild and of the dragon breed.*
> *He swoops all-conquering, borne on airy wing,*
> *With fire and sword he makes his harvesting;*
> *Trembles before him Jove [Zeus], whom gods so dread,*
> *And quakes the darksome river of the dead. (Neumann, 1971, p. 7)*

So, Psyche put on a wedding gown and went to the crag. Her parents were in grief but thought they had to obey the oracle and the heavens. Psyche was afraid but consoled them. They left her there, and, as she waited in fear and trembling on the summit of the crag, a soft breeze from the West raised her and let her fall gently down onto the earth.

Psyche fell asleep, and when she was rested, she woke to find a palace in the heart of a grove and beside a stream. It was made of gold and silver and full of jewels of every kind of splendor. Disembodied voices told her all this wealth was hers and that they were her servants and would give her whatever she needed.

When night came, so did her husband, and he climbed into bed with her and made Psyche his bride. He departed before dawn, before it became light enough for her to see him. This went on for a very long time.

Meanwhile, Psyche's parents were growing old and feeble. Her sisters learned of their parents' condition and left their kingdoms to visit. They all grieved Psyche's death, and the two sisters went to the crag and called to her. Eros had known this would happen and told Psyche not to answer their calls. She agreed, but then became very depressed. She wouldn't eat or bathe; she slept all the time and cried ceaselessly. So, Eros told her to go ahead and obey her heart, but he warned her not to tell her sisters anything about him. Psyche agreed and rained on him kisses and sweet words.

So, the West Wind bore her sisters down from the crag. They saw the palace and the wealth in which Psyche lived and became envious. During their conversation, Psyche answered one of the questions about her husband and said he was young and handsome with a beard of down. Then, she stopped herself and sent them away with gifts before other questions came.

The sisters were more envious—one had a husband older than their father; he was feeble and held the house under lock and key. The other's husband was sick and old and cared nothing for love—she was his sick-nurse and not a lover. When the sisters talked about their experience with Psyche at the palace, they said she was haughty and arrogant and did not want them there, pushing them out as soon as she could. They became more envious and planned Psyche's destruction.

The second time the sisters wanted to come visit, Psyche again convinced Eros, and he again warned her of their destructive intentions. Psyche assured him she could handle things, and the West Wind again brought the sisters down from the crag. By this time, Psyche was pregnant, and the sisters became more envious. This time, Psyche made up a new story about her husband in answer to one of the questions. With this, the sisters realized she had never seen him and concluded that he must be a god. So, they devised a plan.

The third time the sisters visited Psyche, they told her that her husband was a serpent—they reminded her of the oracle that had stated she would marry a beast. They warned Psyche that her serpent husband would devour her and her child and told her that, to prevent this, she should take a razor and lamp, conceal them in the bedroom, and then, when her husband had fallen asleep, she should light the lamp, take the razor, and cut his head from his body. Then, the sisters left.

Psyche was terribly afraid her sisters were right, especially since she had not been allowed to see Eros—only to feel him. So, she got ready with the plan. When Eros was asleep, she lit the lamp with razor in hand, ready to kill him, but instead she saw that he was a god. She dropped the razor and lamented her plan. She picked up one of his arrows and tested its tip on her finger—she cut herself, and then fell in love with Love. She kissed Eros, and the lamp began to spew oil. The oil landed on Eros's shoulder, burning and awakening him. He saw that Psyche had lit the lamp to see him even though he had told her not to do so, and, with that betrayal, he flew off. Psyche held onto his leg as he flew ever higher. Then, she could hold on no longer and fell to the earth. She watched Eros disappear and was so distraught that she flung herself into the river to die. The river, however, laid her unhurt on its bank.

It just so happened the god Pan was nearby with Echo. Pan called to Psyche, as he knew her plight, and told her with gentle words to pray to Eros and win him back by submission.

So, Psyche began to search for Eros.

On the way, she called on her first sister and told her what had happened and that Eros was a god and not a serpent. She added that he had mentioned to Psyche that he wanted to marry her sister. The sister ran to the crag immediately and flung herself off, thinking the West Wind would carry her down to the palace. It did not, and she fell brutally to her death.

Psyche confronted the second sister with the same story, and she also fell to her death.

While this was going on, a sea bird flew down into the ocean and told Aphrodite what had happened. Also, it told her that since Eros had been wounded and Aphrodite had been under the sea, there was no pleasure or joy on earth. Wedlock and true friendship and parents' love for children had vanished. There was nothing but one vast disorder—hateful loathing of all bonds of love.

Aphrodite was angry and raging. She was ready to punish Eros and to kill Psyche.

She met Demeter and Hera as she left to deliver her punishment. They saw her rage and calmed her by reminding her of Eros' age and that his sin was nothing more than falling for the very love for which Aphrodite is known.

During this time, Psyche had continued her search for Eros and found Demeter's altar. She paid homage to Demeter and begged her to protect her. Demeter came to her and said no, that she could not betray her kinswoman, Aphrodite.

Psyche then found Hera's altar and prayed for Hera to save her. Again, no.

So, Psyche, who now felt hopeless and left adrift, sought the answer within herself and decided to submit to Aphrodite.

The first to meet Psyche at the door was one of Aphrodite's servants, Habit, who scolded her and dragged her by the hair to face Aphrodite. Aphrodite confronted her in a rage and accused Psyche of being promiscuous and nothing more than a servant. Then she turned Psyche over to her handmaidens, Trouble and Sorrow, who tortured and tormented her before turning her back over to their mistress. Psyche was far along in her pregnancy, and Aphrodite told her that her child would be a bastard son since there was no legitimate wedding and the parties were not of equal birth.

Then, she set the first task to Psyche: Aphrodite heaped into a huge pile seeds, peas, lentils, and beans and bade Psyche prove her worth by sorting the seeds by nightfall. Feeling overwhelmed, Psyche sat silent and stupefied. Pitying her, an ant called on the host of ants in the vicinity, and they separated the grains. When Aphrodite returned that evening, she angrily suggested the separation was done by Eros, who was healing from his wound somewhere in the house.

So, she gave Psyche a second task: gathering a wisp of wool from sheep whose fleece shone like gold. Psyche rose, intending to relieve her woes by casting herself off a cliff that overhung the river. But a green reed from the riverbed told Psyche not to pollute its river by slaying herself. It warned Psyche of the noonday sun's effect on the sheep, infusing them with fierce madness and anger, and it alerted her to the sharpness of the sheep's horns, the hardness of their foreheads, and the venom of their bites. The reed advised her to wait until the sheep left the shade of the tree and then gather the wool left behind on the twigs, so Psyche did so. Again, Aphrodite attributed Psyche's completion of the task to Eros.

Aphrodite's third trial tested Psyche's "'stout heart and prudence beyond the prudence of woman'" (Neumann, 1971, p. 44). She told Psyche she must use a small crystal jar to draw icy water from the high summit of a mountain from which the black stream flows down to flood the Stygian swamps and feed the streams of Cocytus. Psyche went to the peak of that mountain, assuring herself that if all else failed, she could put an end to her miserable existence. From the jaws of the monstrous rock where the stream burst forth, Psyche noticed the narrow channel worn for its path. To the right and left, from crannies in the crag, crept forth fierce dragons whose eyes keep unending watch. Even the waters forbade approach and warned of death, leaving Psyche overwhelmed and as powerless as if she had been turned to stone, unable to even weep. An eagle, Zeus's royal bird, came to Psyche's aid. As even the gods swore by the majesty of Styx, Psyche gave the eagle the jar, and it braved the dragons and told the waters it sought them at Aphrodite's bidding. Psyche received the full jar with joy and returned it to Aphrodite, who was unappeased.

The final task: Aphrodite gave Psyche a box and directed her to the Underworld to get from Persephone a portion of her beauty sufficient to last Aphrodite just one day, for her beauty had perished through watching over her sick son. Psyche knew she was being driven to her death, for she was constrained by her own feet to tread her way to Tartarus and the spirits of the dead. She went to a high tower that she might throw herself from it, but the tower cried out and stopped her from slaying herself and collapsing before this last of her perils. The tower told her of a path to the Underworld palace where Persephone resides, instructing her to bring in each hand a cake of barley and mead and in her mouth to carry two coins. It explained what to do with the coins and cakes; informed her not to take pity or give aid along the way down; and advised her what to eat at Persephone's welcoming feast and to take her humble place seated on the ground. Finally, the tower warned Psyche not to open or look within the box of divine beauty on her return. Psyche followed all of the instructions, but upon returning with the box of Persephone's beauty into the light of day, she opened the box and found there was nothing in it except a deep sleep that then fell upon Psyche. Eros, who had recovered from his wound, went to Psyche and wiped the sleep from her and back into the box where it belonged. He then told Psyche to complete the task and take the box to his mother, and he soared to Olympus.

While Psyche was returning the box to Aphrodite, Eros spoke to Zeus to ask for his aid. Zeus had gathered together all of the gods and goddesses and announced the heavenly marriage of Eros and Psyche, sending Hermes to get Psyche and bring her to heaven. When he did, Zeus offered her a goblet of ambrosia to drink and, thus, become immortal—which she did. A great nuptial banquet was held, and soon Psyche gave birth to their child, a daughter they named Pleasure.

References

Introduction, Marilyn Marshall

Jung, C. G. (2009). *The red book: Liber novus*. (M. Kyburz, J. Peck & S. Shamdasani, Trans.). Mondadori Printing.

McNeely, D. A. (2012). *A Russian lullaby*. Fisher King Press.

Candles in the Sea, Constance Romero

Jung, C. G. (1989). *Memories, dreams, reflections*. Vintage Books. (Original published in 1961)

Love Letters, Carolyn Bates

Hemingway, E. (1929). A farewell to arms. Jonathan Cape Publishers.

King James Bible. (2017). King James Bible Online. https://www.kingjamesbibleonline.org/ (Original work published 1769)

I Still Listen for Her Voice, Nancy Qualls-Corbett

Jung, C. G. (1969). On the nature of the psyche (R. F. C. Hull, Trans.). In H. Read et al. (Eds.), *The collected works of C. G. Jung: Vol. 8. Structure and dynamics of the psyche* (2nd ed., pp. 159-234). Princeton University Press. (Original work published 1954) https://doi.org/10.1515/9781400850952.159

Jung, C. G. (1970). *The collected works of C. G. Jung: Vol. 14. Mysterium coniunctionis* (R. F. C. Hull, Trans.) (H. Read et al., Eds.). Princeton University Press. (Original work published 1955-56) https://doi.org/10.1515/9781400850853

Ulanov, A. B. (1971). *The feminine in Jungian psychology and in Christian theology*. Northwestern University Press.

A Love Story, Susan Clements Negley

Jung, C. G. (1970). *The collected works of C. G. Jung: Vol. 14. Mysterium coniunctionis* (R. F. C. Hull, Trans.) (H. Read et al., Eds.). Princeton University Press. (Original work published 1955-56) https://doi.org/10.1515/9781400850853

Jung, C. G. (1968). *The collected works of C. G. Jung: Vol. 09 pt. 2. Aion: Researches into the phenomenology of the self* (R. F. C. Hull, Trans.) (H. Read et al., Eds.). Princeton University Press. (Original work published 1951) https://doi.org/10.1515/9781400851058

Jung, C. G. (1969). Archetypes of the collective unconscious (R. F. C. Hull, Trans.). In H. Read et al. (Eds.), *The collected works of C. G. Jung: Vol. 9 pt. 1. Archetypes and the collective unconscious* (2nd ed., pp. 3-41). Princeton University Press. (Original work published 1954) https://doi.org/10.1515/9781400850969.3

Marshall, M. (2005). A 'close-up' of the kiss. *Spring*, *73*, 118-132.

Qualls-Corbett, N. (1988). *The sacred prostitute*. Inner City Books.

Rūmī, J.-D. (1995). *The essential Rumi*. (C. Barks, Trans.). New York, New York: HarperCollins.

The Holy Bible, *Book of wisdom*, chapter 7.

The Holy Bible, *Ezekiel*, chapter 16.

The Holy Bible, *Genesis*, chapter 2.

Winwood, S. (1969). Can't find my way home [Song recorded by Blind Faith]. On *The summer of '69 (Hyde Park FM)* [Album]. Cult Legends.

Wrye, H. K., & Welles, J. K. (1998). *The narration of desire: Erotic transferences and countertransferences*. Routledge.

Eros and the Stranger, Janice Quinn

Camus, A. (1989). *The stranger*. Vintage. (Original work published 1946)

Delaney, B. (2021, October 21). I locked eyes with a stranger crossing the street and felt the blast of pure eros. *The Guardian*. https://www.theguardian.com/commentisfree/2021/oct/22/i-locked-eyes-with-a-stranger-crossing-the-street-and-felt-the-blast-of-pure-eros

Jung, C. G. (1978). *C. G. Jung speaking: Interviews and encounters* (W. McGuire & R. F. C. Hull, Eds.). Princeton University Press.

Jung, C. G. (1989). *Memories, dreams, reflections* (A. Jaffé, Ed.). (R. Winston & C. Winston, Trans.). Vintage Books. (Original work published 1961)

New King James Bible. (2004-2024). Bible Hub. https://biblehub.com/nkjv/1_corinthians/13.htm/ (Original work published 1979)

The Philoctetes Center. (2008, October 14). *The Poetry of Eros*. The Philoctetes Center for the Multidisciplinary Study of the Imagination. http://www.philoctetes.org/past_programs/the_poetry_of_eros

Training in Love, Marilyn Marshall

de Loyola, I. L. (1992). *The spiritual exercises of St. Ignatius*. (G. Ganss, Trans.). Loyola Press. (Original work published 1548)

Jung, C. G. (1967). *The collected works of C. G. Jung: Vol. 5. Symbols of transformation* (R. F. C. Hull, Trans.) (H. Read et al., Eds.). Princeton University Press. (Original work published 1952) https://doi.org/10.1515/9781400850945

Jung, C. G. (1970). *The collected works of C. G. Jung: Vol. 14. Mysterium coniunctionis* (R. F. C. Hull, Trans.) (H. Read et al., Eds.). Princeton University Press. (Original work published 1955-56) https://doi.org/10.1515/9781400850853

Jung, C. G. (1971). *The collected works of C. G. Jung: Vol. 6. Psychological types* (R. F. C. Hull, Trans.) (H. Read et al., Eds.). Princeton University Press. (Original work published 1921) https://doi.org/10.1515/9781400850860

Kerényi, C. (1980). *The gods of the Greeks*. Thames and Hudson, Inc.

Rodney, E. (Producer). (1954–1960). *Father knows best* [TV Series]. Screen Gems; Columbia Pictures Television.

Vogel, K. & Noble, V. (1981). *Motherpeace round tarot deck*. U.S. Games Systems, Inc.

The Healing of Medusa: A Dream Journey, Barbara Friedman

Adittapariyaya Sutta: The fire sermon. (1993.) (T. Bhikkhu, Trans.). Retrieved from Access to Insight Website: https://www.accesstoinsight.org/tipitaka/sn/sn35/sn35.028.than.html

Alagaddupama Sutta. (2004). (T. Bhikhu, Trans.). Retrieved from Access to Insight Website: https://www.accesstoinsight.org/tipitaka/mn/mn.022.than.html

Brensilver, M. [AudioDharma]. (2024, November 6). *Dharmette: Post-election reflections* [Audio file]. Retrieved from https://www.audiodharma.org/talks/21671

Campbell, J. (1976). *Occidental mythology: the masks of God*. Penguin Books.

Downing, C. (1990). Only the wounded healer heals: The testimony of Greek mythology. *Soundings: An Interdisciplinary Journal, 73*(4), 551–573.

Edinger, E. F. (1985). *Anatomy of the psyche*. Open Court Publishing Co.

Eisler, R. (1987). *The chalice & the blade: Our history, our future*. Harper Collins.

Epstein, M. (2014). *The trauma of everyday life*. Penguin Books.

Evslin, B. (1987). *Medusa (Monsters of mythology)*. Chelsea House Publishers.

George, V. (1986). *The history of the goddess and the transpersonal significance of her decline and re-emergence in the west*. Ann Arbor, Michigan, University Microfilms.

Gimbutas, M. (2001). *The living goddesses*. University of California Press.

Google. (2024). *Tao te ching Lao-Tse*, text generated by Google AI overview, Generative.

Graves, R. (1957). *The Greek myths* (Vol. 1). Penguin Books.

Grimm, C. (2013). *Grimm's fairy tales*. Catwell Books.

Hamilton, E. (1969). *Mythology: Timeless tales of gods and heroes*. Penguin Books.

Perera, S. (1981). *Descent to the goddess*. Inner City Books.

Rilke, R. M. (2021). *Letters to a young poet: A new translation and commentary* (A. Barrows & J. Macy, Trans.). Shambhala Publications, Inc. (Original work published 1929)

The Adittapariyaya Sutta (The discourse on everything being aflame), in the *Saṃyutta Nikāya* (The connected discourses of the Buddha). (2000). (B. Bodhi, Trans.). Wisdom Publications.

The Alagaddūpama Sutta (The simile of the snake), in the *Majjhima Nikāya* (The middle length discourses of the Buddha). (1995). (B. Ñāṇamoli & B. Bodhi, Trans.). Wisdom Publications.

The Holy Bible: New Revised Standard Version Catholic Edition. (1990). Oxford University Press.

The King James Bible. (2004/1611). Hendrickson Publishers.

von Franz M-L. (1974). *Shadow and evil in fairy tales*. Shambhala Press.

West, M. (2016). *Into the darkest places: Early relational trauma and borderline states of mind*. Karnac Books.

Liberated by Love, Jacqueline Wright

Grimm, J. and Grimm, W. (1944). *The complete Grimm's fairy tales*. Pantheon Books, Inc. (Original work published 1812)

Jung, C. G. (1966). The relations between the ego and the unconscious (R. F. C. Hull, Trans.). In H. Read et al. (Eds.), *The collected works of C. G. Jung: Vol. 7. Two essays on analytical psychology* (2nd ed., pp. 121–241). Princeton University Press. (Original work published 1928) https://doi.org/10.1515/9781400850891.121

Neumann, E. (1956). *Amor and Psyche*. Bolligen Foundation, Inc. (Original work published 1952)

Oliver, M. (2020). *Devotions*. Penguin Books.

Rilke, R. M. (1954). *Letters to a young poet.* W. W. Norton & Company. (Original work published 1929)

Rūmī, J.-D. (1995). *The essential Rumi.* (C. Barks, Trans.). HarperCollins.

Singer, J. (1988). *Modern woman in search of a soul.* Nicolas-Hays, Inc.

In Her Honor, Marilyn Marshall

Jung, C. G. (1970). Flying saucers: A modern myth of things seen in the skies (R. F. C. Hull, Trans.). In H. Read et al. (Eds.), *The collected works of C. G. Jung: Vol. 10. Civilization in transition* (2nd ed., pp. 307-433). Princeton University Press. (Original work published 1958) https://doi.org/10.1515/9781400850976.307

A Summary of the Eros and Psyche Myth, Marilyn Marshall

Apuleius, L. (1998). *The golden ass: Metamorphoses of Lucius Apuleius* (E. Kenney, Trans.). Penguin Classics. (Original work published c. 160)

Neumann, E. (1956). *Amor and Psyche: The psychic development of the feminine: A commentary on the tale by Apuleius*. (R. Manheim, Trans.). Princeton University Press. (Original work published in 1952)

Additional Resources from the Authors

Jungian Terminology

Sharp, D. (1991). *C. G. Jung lexicon: A primer of terms and concepts*. Inner City Books.

The Feminine and the Goddess

Dorsey, L. (2020). *Orishas, goddesses, and voodoo queens: The divine feminine in the African religious traditions*. Weiser Books.

Gimbutas, M. (1989). *The language of the goddess: Unearthing the hidden symbols of western civilization*. Harper & Row, Publishers, Inc.

Graves, R. (2011). *The Greek myths: The complete and definitive edition*. Penguin UK. (Original work published 1955)

Harding, M. E. (1973). *Psychic energy: Its source and its transformation*. Princeton University Press.

Leonard, L. S. (1982). *The wounded woman: Healing the father-daughter relationship*. Shambhala.

Luke, H. M. (1996). *The way of woman: Awakening the perennial feminine*. PRH Christian Publishing.

Murray, A. S. (2014). *Manual of mythology: Greek and Roman, Norse and Old German, Hindoo and Egyptian mythology*. HardPress Publishing. (Original work published 1895)

Raff, J. (2003). *The wedding of Sophia: The divine feminine in psychoidal alchemy*. Nicolas-Hays, Inc.

Ulanov, A. B. (1981). *Receiving woman: Studies in the psychology and theology of the feminine*. Daimon Verlag. (Original work published 1981)

Active Imagination

Jung, C. G. (1989). *Jung on active imagination* (J. Chodorow, Ed.). Routledge.

Buddhism

Epstein, M. (2013). *Thoughts without a thinker: Psychotherapy from a Buddhist perspective*. Basic Books. (Original work published 1995)

Goldstein, J. (2016). *Mindfulness: A practical guide to awakening*. Sounds True. (Original work published 2013)

Kornfield, J. (Ed.). (1993). *Teachings of the Buddha*. Shambhala.

Welwood, J. (2002). *Toward a psychology of awakening: Buddhism, psychotherapy, and the path of personal and spiritual transformation*. Shambhala.

About the Authors

Carolyn Bates

Carolyn Bates, PhD, is a Jungian analyst practicing in Austin, Texas, and, at the time of publication, is the North American Editor-in-Chief for the *Journal of Analytical Psychology*. She is a training analyst with the Inter-Regional Society of Jungian Analysts. Over the last three decades she has presented internationally on the ethics of treatment boundaries, technology's influence within the collective, the phenomena of synchronicity and collective trauma, the reconsideration of myth through the lens of feminist politics, and the epidemic of gun violence in the United States. She has published in the *Journal of Analytical Psychology*, *Psychological Perspectives*, *Archive for Research in Archetypal Symbolism*, and the British Psychoanalytic Council's *New Associations* magazine. She has performed as Eve in her two-person staged reading, *Eve Speaks: A Mythopoetic Dialogue on the Deconstruction of Privilege*, and with the IRSJA Players in staged readings penned by her colleagues: *Visions of Genius: Jung, Joyce, Lucia* (author, Deldon Anne McNeely); *The Red Book: Opening the Vault of the Heart* (authors, Constance Romero and Marilyn Marshall). She has long been a proponent of permaculture and, during the worst of the Covid-19 pandemic, found refuge and joy in looking back through history to best understand how to establish a Victory Garden in her backyard, an endeavor that underscored for her the necessity of harmonious relationships with nature. Contact: drbatesaustin@gmail.com

Barbara Friedman

Barbara Friedman, PhD, is a clinical psychologist and a Jungian psychoanalyst in private practice in Chicago, Illinois. She is a graduate of the Inter-Regional Society of Jungian Analysts. Barbara is a senior teaching analyst and has served as president of the C. G. Jung Institute of Chicago. Her postgraduate training includes The Institute for Meditation and Psychotherapy and The Center for Mindfulness and Compassion through the Cambridge Health Alliance and Harvard Medical School. Barbara is a long-time student of Eastern philosophy and religion, particularly Buddhism. Her writing and lectures connect Jungian studies and Buddhist practice as well as feminism. In her book, *Partners in Healing: Redistributing the Power in the Counselor/Client Relationship*, she examines the power dynamic in the therapeutic relationship. Contact: bfriedman14@gmail.com

Marilyn Marshall

Marilyn Marshall, MA, LPC, is a Jungian psychoanalyst in private practice in New Orleans, Louisiana. She is a Senior Training Analyst in the Inter-Regional Society of Jungian Analysts (IRSJA), a member of the International Association of Analytical Psychology, and a faculty member and past coordinator for the New Orleans Jungian Seminar. Marilyn facilitates case colloquia and presents lectures and seminars with a particular focus on sexuality and spirituality in the Psyche and Eros myth. She is coauthor of *The Red Book: Opening the Vault of the Heart,* a play adapted from Jung's *The Red Book* and presented at IRSJA and IAAP conferences, Jung societies and training seminars. Publications include articles, case commentaries, and reviews in *Spring Journal*, the *Journal of Analytical Psychology*, and *Psychological Perspectives*. Contact: marilynjmarshall@gmail.com

Susan Clements Negley

Susan Clements Negley, MA, LPC, is a Jungian psychoanalyst in San Antonio, Texas. She is a member of the Inter-Regional Society of Jungian Analysts and a training analyst for the Texas Seminar. Her articles and book reviews, including topics such as the persona, postpartum depression, shamanism, and the culinary and visual arts, have been published in *Psychological Perspectives*, *The Jung Journal*, and the *Journal of Humanistic Psychology*. She has the Grand Diplôme from Le Cordon Bleu Ecole de Cuisine and has written and presented extensively on her past career as a professional chef. Her thesis, *The Coniunctio Gastronomique: A Study of the Individuation Process in Culinary Terms*, is being adapted into book form. She is also currently working on an essay about her experience with and recovery from post-traumatic stress after witnessing the aftermath on the day of the school shooting in Uvalde, Texas. Contact: scnegley@gmail.com

Nancy Qualls-Corbett

Nancy Qualls-Corbett, PhD, is a Jungian analyst in private practice (now retired) in Birmingham, Alabama. She holds a diploma from the C. G. Jung Institute - Zürich in Zürich, Switzerland. She held several positions with the Inter-Regional Society of Jungian Analysts on their executive, review, admission, and ethics committees and served on the faculty at the New Orleans Jungian Seminar. She is the author of two books, *The Sacred Prostitute: Eternal Aspect of the Feminine* (1988) and *Awakening Woman: Dreams and Individuation* (with Leila McMackin, 2002). An interview with Dr. Qualls-Corbett appears in Volume 2 of *Living with Jung: "Enterviews" with Jungian Analysts*, by Robert and Janis Henderson, and her essay, "Redeeming the Feminine: Eros and the World Soul," is found in *The Dream and Its Amplification*, edited by Erel Shalit and Nancy Swift Furlotti. She has lectured throughout the United States and, with her love of travel, has led seminar groups in Greece, Egypt, France, and Italy, as well as visiting the sacred places of Mary Magdalene, Dionysus, and the Villa of Mysteries. Contact: nlcq32@gmail.com

Janice Quinn

Janice Quinn, PhD, LCSW, MPA, MA, is a Jungian analyst with a private practice in Arlington, Virginia, serving the Washington, DC, metropolitan area. She holds a diploma in analytical psychology from the C. G. Jung Institute - Zürich in Zürich, Switzerland. Her thesis was on feminine self-worth. She has masters' degrees in social work from Virginia Commonwealth University, in public administration from Harvard University, and in musicology from the Eastman School of Music. She is a member of the faculty of the Inter-Regional Society of Jungian Analysts and the International Association of Analytical Psychology. She is also a member and past president of the Jungian Analysts of Washington Association (JAWA). She was a Senior Policy Analyst for the U. S. Environmental Protection Agency (USEPA) and also worked for the U. S. Department of State in Washington, D. C. She taught music in Louisville, Kentucky, and has lectured extensively on music and Jung, on *The Red Book*, and on feminine self-worth. She has conducted research in the nexus between spirituality, creativity, and depression. She enjoys singing in her local choral group and is an avid swimmer. She also loves exploring different cultures and has built a French double-manual harpsichord which she plays daily. Contact: janicequinn12@gmail.com

Constance Romero

Constance Romero, MEd, LPC, is a Jungian analyst practicing in New Orleans, Louisiana, and Brevard, North Carolina. She is a Senior Training Analyst with the Inter-Regional Society of

Jungian Analysts and a core faculty member of the New Orleans Jungian Seminar. Connie facilitates dream groups for the public and provides colloquia and individual consultation for analytic candidates. For the last thirty years, she has worked combining her professional experience as an actor/director (former member of SAG-AFTRA) with her love of depth psychology, feminism, and the divine feminine. She is the creator of "Mining Character, Mending the Soul," an experiential program where participants "play" with shadow elements and work toward the healing of trauma. She has directed and coauthored dramatic readings for colleagues and seminars throughout the U. S., Europe, and Indonesia. She currently coedits the "Clinical Commentaries" and "Film & Culture" features for the *Journal of Analytical Psychology* and has published essays and reviews in the *Journal of Analytical Psychology*, *Psychological Perspectives*, and the *International Journal of Jungian Studies*.

Jacqueline Wright

Jacqueline Wright, EdD, resides in Atlanta, Georgia, where she maintains a private practice as a Jungian analyst. She received her diploma in analytical psychology from the C. G. Jung Institute - Zürich. She is a long-standing member of the Inter-Regional Society of Jungian Analysts and a training analyst on the faculties of the Memphis-Atlanta Jungian Seminar and the New Orleans Jungian Seminar. Her background is in education, and, before she began her studies of analytical psychology, she was engaged in a nationwide higher education project, working with colleges and universities in the Mid-South to help them develop programs to improve the quality of learning opportunities for adults returning to college. Her early years of living in the world of storytelling and music in the western North Carolina mountains ignited and fostered her love of myth, fairy tales, folk tales, and folk music.

Other current interests include the role of love in analysis, the archetype of home, the limitations on women's freedoms, and the importance of women speaking their truth about their lives so that real change can happen. Contact: jacquiewright1@gmail.com

www.ingramcontent.com/pod-product-compliance
Lightning Source LLC
LaVergne TN
LVHW052315200926
848481LV00002B/573
* 9 7 8 1 6 8 5 0 3 6 4 8 5 *